TRANSFORMATIONAL TIPS

TRANSFORMATIONAL TIPS

mastering the moments

Theresa A. Gale and Mary Anne Wampler

ISBN: 1979002185
ISBN 13: 9781979002189

Contents

Introduction

Like clockwork, each and every Monday morning since 2011, we have delivered a message on personal and business success that we felt was relevant and thought provoking for that particular week. We fondly named these messages our Monday Morning Tips.

As we celebrate our twenty-first year in business, we have looked back and picked some of our favorites on personal mastery that remain pertinent today and, most likely, tomorrow. We've kept the tips in chronological order here, but no worries; there is an index where you can easily explore specific topics.

In 2018, we will be sporting a new look and feel. Keep your eye out for Transformation Tuesday! It's fresh, inspirational, and will help keep you achieving, moving forward, creating the business and life you've always envisioned.

WE STRIVE TO EMBODY WHAT WE TEACH

If you've known us for a long time, you will see reflected in these tips our own personal stories about growth and development. That's what's so great about our work—it pushes us to grow and develop, so when we ask our clients to consider their growth, we understand the journey it takes and the process that needs to be in place to help them achieve what is most important to them.

If you are reading this book and have no idea who we are, welcome to our unique corner of the world! Transform, Inc., was launched in 1996 by Mary Anne and Theresa, who came together to deliver unprecedented results to our clients. We're often asked, "How did you come up with your name?" Some companies spend thousands of dollars and weeks, if not months, coming up with a name. Not us! Sitting in a restaurant after a visit with a potential client, we took out a bar napkin and started brainstorming. Within thirty minutes, we had it—Transform, Inc. Our name says it all!

Since that day our partnership has thrived, and now, twenty-one years later, we are more committed than ever to transforming businesses and individuals so that they can achieve the levels of success they desire. To learn more about us, visit our website at www.transforminc.com.

WHAT'S OUR SECRET SAUCE?

It really comes down to a few things: our commitment to our own personal growth and development; the depth of our individual expertise; our devotion to discovering the best new, innovative ideas; and, of course, our pioneering use and continuing study and application of the Enneagram in business, which grounds us in our work with organizations, clients, and their employees.

For real transformation to occur, understanding yourself—from the inside out—is paramount. In the first chapter, we explain our Self-Mastery Model, which we have used for ourselves as well as with clients for the last twenty-one years. In the second chapter, we provide a description of the Enneagram. This has been by far the most transformative tool we have used personally and with organizations and individuals. It provides the content (thoughts, feelings, and sensations) that informs self-awareness. These two tools are now ingrained in the work we do, and you'll see them reflected in the tips that follow in the rest of the book.

GRATITUDE— *YAY, TEAM!*

Over the years, we have worked with many individuals who have helped us deliver the Monday Morning Tips to our readers. We'd like to thank Emily Dorr, Kelsey McManimon, and the team at Jean Peterson Design for their creative energy; Tibetha Owen, who edits and assists; Elizabeth Thomas, who insists we produce timely and relevant content; Beth Schillaci, from VillageWorks Communications, Inc., who preceded Elizabeth; and Chris Lachance, who has worked many hours to pull this book together.

Most importantly, we are grateful to our clients, who over the years have been committed to their own personal growth and development and are willing to invest in their employees' personal mastery because they understand that their employees are their greatest asset. It is the partnerships we have with our clients that we value the most. Thank you!

Self-Mastery as a Way of Life

Old habits die hard, as the saying goes. And one habit that most of us share—and find difficult to both notice and shake—is our tendency to run on automatic. Unconscious patterns of thinking, feeling, and behaving are often the silent saboteurs of self-mastery in our personal and professional lives.

For example, a financial adviser is very clear that she must spend 60 percent of her day on the phone with clients if she is to retain their business and get necessary referrals. Yet she is continually attracted to working on less important administrative tasks. A president of a remodeling company has a very long list of projects but is easily distracted when employee and client issues arise, keeping him from finishing any of his projects. His list stays long, his employees stay dependent, and he is continually frustrated. A pediatrician who prides herself on being in control of her life now finds her newly established practice growing so fast that both she and her practice are out of control. She's overwhelmed and unsure. Her pride has been punctured, and now she is angry that she has lost control of managing herself, her business, and her staff.

Until we uncover and recognize patterns that have become habitual, we cannot achieve mastery—that state of being where actions are guided by awareness and intention rather than habit and reaction. Many times, we automatically act before we apply any awareness to situations, and then we regret our actions or are unaware of their impact on others and ourselves. The key to mastery is the level of consciousness we bring to our thoughts, emotions, our physical presence, and our actions. Developing this level of awareness is a skill that can and must be learned if we are to achieve any level of mastery within desired areas of our personal and professional life.

As we move toward mastery, the results are compelling, rewarding, and powerful. At each of the seven levels of the mastery model, new discoveries are made that can positively impact how we feel about ourselves and the people around us and how we react to and shape certain situations. For business leaders, self-mastery is a valuable tool that shapes results, daily quality-of-life issues, and helps gain skills necessary to become the leaders that will take us and our organizations into a bright and visionary future.

KEY ELEMENTS OF THE MASTERY MODEL

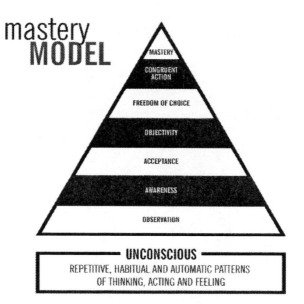

1. OBSERVATION

The journey toward self-mastery begins with observing a situation or interaction. Keep in mind that observation is a learned skill that gets easier and refined with practice. You may find at first that your observations occur at the end of the day as you reflect upon situations you encountered. Other observations may come in the form of feedback from your colleagues. As you become more comfortable with this skill, you will find yourself observing more "in the moment" rather than after the fact.

2. AWARENESS

Once you begin observing, you can tune into your habitual patterns of thinking, feeling, and behaving and their influence over your emotions and actions. For example, the president of the remodeling company mentioned earlier realizes that he believes other people's issues are more important than his own. He thinks, "If I just deal with their issue now, I can get back to my work." The reality is that by addressing these issues immediately, he unconsciously encourages people to continually bring their issues to him—thus keeping him from doing his work. The result is that he ends up staying late into the night working just to stay on top of his task list. Awareness helps us discover the *why* behind what we do. Once we understand the why, we are ready for the next step—acceptance.

3. ACCEPTANCE

Knowing why we do what we do leads us to realize that we have not been in control but rather on automatic, acting from habit, faulty beliefs, or assumptions. This realization may be a difficult one to swallow, yet accepting what "is" right now is the launching pad toward self-mastery. Acceptance without self-critical judgments, knowing that we have always done the very best we could, is important and opens the door to the next step of mastery.

4. OBJECTIVITY

Now that you're observing and aware and able to understand and accept why you do what you do, you can step back and objectively assess a situation or interaction. Is your approach—formulated by your habitual patterns of thinking, feeling, and behaving—producing the desired results? Or is it time to choose a different course of action? In the instance of the president of the remodeling company, he was no longer willing to work hours into the night and realized it was time to choose a different strategy.

5. FREEDOM TO CHOOSE

You have arrived at the crossroads. When you're on automatic, there is no freedom of choice. But now you recognize the unconscious habits that drive you—and you can consciously choose your behavior and response. For the financial adviser mentioned previously, this newfound freedom of choice may empower him to establish times when he will be available for administrative tasks. The pediatrician may establish clearly defined roles and responsibilities for her staff, stop doing administrative tasks that her staff should be doing, hold her staff accountable for the results, and let go of the belief that she has to micromanage in order to stay in control. She may choose instead to meet weekly with staff members and review a series of management reports that inform her of the state of the business.

6. CONGRUENT ACTION

Choosing the next right action and doing it are two different animals. Intellectually we often know the right action to take, but old beliefs may inhibit us from doing them. A salesperson knows intellectually that right action for her is to ask the client for a referral, but when she gets in front of the client, she can't get the words out of her mouth. Congruent action means that you choose to act in a certain way and you do it! As you master certain skills, this way of being becomes effortless and automatic.

7. MASTERY

Congratulations! You've crossed the finish line. But remember that mastery is an ongoing process, a continuous practice that is available to all yet utilized effectively by few. As you continue to develop and refine the skills, behaviors, and attitudes that reinforce mastery, you will achieve your desired results and recognize the positive, productive impact on those around you.

Theresa Gale and Mary Anne Wampler

2

The Enneagram Advantage

JANUARY 2011

Study and use of the Enneagram in organizations significantly impacts both personal and organizational results. This cutting-edge technology describes nine distinct personality styles that have a distinctive way of thinking, acting, and being. Each style has its own natural gifts, limitations, blind spots, and approaches to communication, decision making, teamwork, leadership, and learning. Understanding the style of coworkers and leaders in the organization dramatically increases communication, productivity, employee morale, and bottom-line results for the organization.

One of the values of this tool lies in its ability to give insight into the why behind behavior. While many of us might have difficulty with time management (the behavior), the reasons why (motivation) each of us has difficulty are most probably different. Many personality systems on the market today, that is, Myers-Briggs, DISC, The Big Five, and so on, while insightful and useful in their own rights, describe or predict behavior that an individual will exhibit. Only the Enneagram goes underneath behavior and reveals motivation. Once an individual understands *why* he or she does what he or she does, then change is possible.

Another value of the Enneagram is that it shatters individual perceptions of other individual's intentions and reasons for acting. The Enneagram teaches that there are nine different "lens" or ways of interpreting the world in which we live. Through this lens or style, each of us interprets situations, events, encounters, and experiences through only one-ninth of the truth. There are eight other ways to view the same situation, and yet, I seem to believe that my interpretation is the "right" interpretation.

The Enneagram helps us understand that in any dialogue, there may be distinctly different points of view. Likewise, how one interprets a situation may not truly reflect the intentions of others, and one may make assumptions and take action based on incomplete information. The end result is that miscommunication, misunderstandings, and inaccurate assumptions get in the way of communicating and working effectively with others.

A third value of the Enneagram lies in its ability to reveal individual barriers to success and to offer a prescriptive path for continuous learning, development, and growth. In learning my style, each of us gains insight into our "lens" of the world, understands what may be missing as we interpret situations, uncovers individual motivations for the way each of us acts and reacts to situations, and reveals the habitual, automatic, and often unconscious responses we resort to on a fairly frequent basis.

How does knowing all this help the employee? Well, the habitual responses we learned and know so well don't always get us the results we want or need. Likewise, our reactions, if unhealthy, may significantly impact how we relate to others and how others relate to us. Knowing our style helps us increase our level of awareness, through self-observation, to these habitual patterns of thinking, acting, reacting, and interacting, and with this awareness, we now have a choice as to how we want to act or be in any given situation or moment. Imagine not having to feel bad, apologetic, or guilty about how you reacted to a person or situation but actually having the awareness and making the choice for how you act in the moment. This is the power of the Enneagram!

Theresa Gale and Mary Anne Wampler

3

Monday Morning Tips

JUNE 20, 2011

Waking Up

Here's what's been "waking me up" this week. Well, it's been a week full of learning for me and hopefully for a few others. There are three themes that are clearly in my awareness this past week. They landed in my heart, where so very many of my personal life lessons land as they transform. These particular lessons have helped my eyes and my heart open wide, and for that I am grateful.

Here's the deal:

1. How we interact with another can have a huge **impact**. Probably more impact than we know. Sometimes it is super positive, some-times it's neutral, and sometimes it's just downright critical. Some people know their impact and "impact away," while others are clueless about how they impact. And, yes, even those of us who are on a path of self-discovery and enlightenment go clue-less from time to time. Yet, the impact is the impact. If we are to be great leaders, or good friends and colleagues, we must learn about our impact and then make solid decisions and be inten-tional as we interact with others.

2. Without moment-by-moment *self-awareness*, old habits take over and can damage relationships for a moment, or forever.

3. *Kindness* never goes out of style. Truth is always a good answer, and the timing of stating your particular view of the truth with someone matters greatly. When sharing something with a colleague, friend, or loved one, please make sure it's the right time, and check out what your intentions are in that particular moment. Sometimes we need to say something right away; however, much can wait until we are clear headed. Words can be powerful. You may want to take what I am now calling a "consideration pause" before you speak to make sure that your message is constructive, helpful, kind, and honest!

Believe me when I say that I really *know* that this growth stuff is at some level simple and not often easy. My hope is that we all learn to get clear, take our time, be reflective, and when we mess up—(because we are all going to), take responsibility for our impact by sharing a heartfelt and honest "I'm sorry!"

Cheers to kindness!

Mary Anne Wampler

AUGUST 1, 2011

Active Listening with Discipline

Active listening requires a disciplined effort to silence
all that internal conversation while we are attempting
to listen to another human being.
~James H.

Active listening requires a disciplined effort. What does that mean? Active listening is just that—active. It means being fully present to another individuals as they speak. By fully present we don't just mean physically present but emotionally and mentally present as well. It's not easy to do this, especially when there are so many distractions tugging at us. Our internal conversations rob us of the ability to communicate the message that we are truly interested in and value what our prospects, clients, coworkers, and loved ones have to say. How active is your internal talk? Notice when your internal talk is planning what you are going to say, thinking about the consequences of your next statement, focused on another project or task, judging the other person, or worrying about something else. Raising your level of awareness is the first step to becoming a more active listener.

The second step is to actively work on dropping the internal chatter when interacting with others. Develop a strategy for releasing your internal talk. Some people imagine a container where they place their thoughts for future access, while others find that just naming the talk helps to drop it in the moment. Whatever strategy you develop, practice it over and over until it becomes habit.

Active listening says what you have to say matters…don't we all want to experience that?

Theresa Gale

OCTOBER 31, 2011

Start Close In

Recently, we were privileged to spend time with David Wythe, a poet, storyteller, and business consultant. Not only is he very charming (with a British accent) but incredibly gifted in his ability to capture the human spirit and story in poetry.

In his poem "Start Close In," he begins:

> *Start close in,*
> *don't take the second step or the third,*
> *start with the first thing close in,*
> *the step you don't want to take.*

Don't we always want to hurry to the end result, skipping past the painful stuff to get to the good stuff?

Wythe urges us to slow down and deal with the "real" issue first. He gives us some clues how to do this. His poem continues:

> *Start with the ground you know,*
> *the pale ground beneath your feet,*
> *your own way of starting the conversation.*
>
> *Start with your own question,*
> *give up on other people's questions,*
> *don't let them smother something simple.*

There you have it: start with what you know, start with yourself, don't look outside yourself or to others, but rather, take time to find you own answers within. It is way too easy to pull out a book, or search the Internet, or call your friends and ask them what to do...what is called for is to stop all the doing, slow down, and listen to what you are saying, feeling, wanting, or know to be right for you.

Take time this week to breathe, listen, and, in the silence, you will find your answers.

Take the first step…not the second or the third…just the first.

Theresa Gale and Mary Anne Wampler

NOVEMBER 13, 2011

Hope Is Not a Strategy

This is the title of a sales book that is about how to win complex sales deals, yet the title lends itself to so many situations that we thought we'd look at it as this week begins.

"Hope motivates virtually all human activity. Hope is the powerhouse internal trigger that automatically helps determine our decisions and our actions" (The 7 Triggers to Yes, Russell Granger).

In interactions with others, hope is powerful…hope that others will change their behaviors or attitudes, or hope that a prospect will buy something from us, or hope that the client will send the payment so that you can make payroll or pay the bills.

Hope, however, without action, is not a strategy; it's just a thought!

If you hope a prospect will buy your product but you don't follow your sales process, then hope is not a strategy. If you hope that the client will send the check and you don't pick up the phone and call to ask where the payment is, then hope is not a strategy. If you hope that an employee shows up for work on time, but you don't have a conversation with the employee when he or she is late, then hope is not a strategy.

Discovering what you or others hope for is powerful, but without action behind it, the result is often disappointment.

What do you hope for this week?

What action will you take to turn your hopes into reality?

Make it a week filled with realized hopes!

Theresa Gale and Mary Anne Wampler

JULY 16, 2012

Challenges and Opportunities: Which Do You See?

Challenge is the core and the mainspring of all human activity.
If there's an ocean, we cross it; if there's a disease, we cure it;
If there's a wrong, we right it; if there's a record, we break it;
and finally, if there's a mountain, we climb it.
~James Ramesy Ullman

Our work with the Enneagram over the years has taught us that we, human beings, don't always see a situation, issue, or interaction the same way. This is due to the fact that we each have a particular lens that we see the world through, and that causes us to interpret life's events differently than others might. The Enneagram describes nine distinctly different lenses that influence how individuals not only see the world but how they think, feel, and act at any given moment.

So, do you see challenges or opportunities? Do you thrive in dealing with challenges, or do you build your life to avoid encountering them? Do you think people who always talk about opportunities, not challenges, are "pie-in-the-sky" dreamers, or do you wish you could see more opportunities rather than challenges? Do you only see opportunities and avoid facing challenges head on?

The point here is not what we think or how we would answer these questions but how you define, handle, and manage opportunities and challenges in your life. Your lens dictates your thoughts, reactions, actions, and results.

- Dare to see challenges as they are, and face them.
- Dare to see opportunities when challenges arise.
- Climb a mountain with both in view, and you'll always reach the top!

Theresa Gale and Mary Anne Wampler

AUGUST 6, 2012

Meditation at Work...Works!

"For 20 years I've been looking for how to add balance to the workplace, and that gave me the idea for the experiment," says David Levy, computer scientist and technology professor at the University of Washington. A student of Zen for twenty years, he knew meditation helped him be more focused and productive at work, but he wanted to find out if this might be true for others.

Levy had one group of human-resource managers undergo eight weeks of mindfulness-based meditation training. A second group got eight weeks of body-relaxation training. The third group received no initial training but then was given the same training as the first group after eight weeks.

Subjects were given a stressful test on their multitasking abilities before and after each eight-week period. They had to use e-mail, calendars, instant-messaging, phones, and Word-processing tools to perform common office duties. Researchers looked at their speed, accuracy, and number of times they switched tasks. The participants also were asked to record their stress levels and memory performance while doing the jobs.

Researchers found that *the meditation group not only had lower stress levels during the multitasking tests but also were able to concentrate longer without being distracted.*

But for the other two groups—those who received relaxation-breathing training and those who had no initial training—stress did not go down. However, when the third group received meditation training after eight weeks, their stress also decreased.

"Further, those who meditated also spent more time on tasks, didn't switch between different chores as often and took no longer to get their work done than the other participants," the study found. *"Meditation is a lot like doing reps at a gym. It strengthens your attention muscle,"* says Levy.

For Mary Anne and I, this has certainly been true in our lives. The more we take ten to twenty minutes a day to sit quietly and do some form of meditation, the more we feel grounded, more focused, and in control. We know that meditation works—the key is to find the right practice and time that works for you. Meditation, also called mindfulness training, means finding ten to twenty minutes to stop all the busyness and sit quietly with yourself. If ten minutes is too much, start with one minute, and work your way up. It's not the length of time you spend; it's the fact that you consistently take time to check in with yourself, let go of your thoughts, and allow some time to just be quiet.

Tony Schwartz, founder of the Energy Project, says we must have time to recharge, or our battery (body) will die (get sick). Meditation, if for only five minutes a day, not only helps to recharge and reenergize us but also increases our focus and performance. Who doesn't want that?

So, we can't help but ask, "What time will you meditate today? Tomorrow?"

Theresa Gale

AUGUST 26, 2012

A Six-Hundred-Mile Uphill and Downhill Journey of a Lifetime

Congratulations to Scott Jamieson, vice president at Bartlett Tree Expert, who recently completed a once-in-a-lifetime adventure. We asked Scott to share with us his journey to the finish line.

I recently participated in a six-hundred–mile, seven-day road cycling fundraising event called the Tour des Trees. This event raises money to identify and fund projects and programs that advance knowledge in the field of arboriculture and urban forestry to benefit people, trees, and the environment.

Seven months of training and three thousand miles on my bike getting ready for the tour was intense and challenging, but nothing really prepared me for what was to come over the six hundred miles road trip. I'd have to say this was the toughest thing I have *ever* done.

As an Enneagram Type 9, I was so aware that I had to keep my eyes fixed on the goal of cycling six hundred miles. Actually, what really motivated me was the goal of completing the ride without ever having to ride in the "sag wagon," and this kept me riding each day in preparation, even on the days I didn't want to ride. Having a clear goal can be tough for me, and yet this event taught me how important goal clarity is for my forward movement. What also kept me going were all the people who donated to my fundraising efforts. The very fact they gave money for the cause in my name gave me that obligation, that commitment to them to complete the task.

Day two of the ride was particularly tough for me, and as I rode alone along the Oregon coast, I thought of the people who contributed to the cause, people who had made encouraging comments, and my family who put up with my long four-hour training rides on the weekends. One "aha moment" along these roads was that I realized that I do best when I am not only doing something for myself but for others as well. Often, I give more for others than perhaps I even do for myself, and that motivated me to keep pedaling.

As a leader, I always lead best when my purpose is clear, the goal is articulated, and I have great people working with me. The Tour des Trees was a great example of that. We rode for nearly one hundred miles each day, and over the seven days, we had thirty thousand in elevation gains. The miles-long climbs of thousands of feet at a time were nearly equally met with exhilarating downhill descents on the other side, where I often reached speeds of forty-three miles per hour as I hurtled past huge Sitka spruces and Douglas firs that lined our Oregon roads.

There might not be an equal amount of down hills for every uphill in life but it is interesting to this Nine how "things always seem to work out." Such is the needed balance when riding a bike and, for me, the balance in this journey we call our life.

By Scott Jamieson, Vice President, Bartlett Tree

SEPTEMBER 17, 2012

Life Is a Series of Hero's Journeys

One evening I was watching the movie *Finding Joe* with a friend. We were thoroughly engrossed in the movie when my twenty-two-year-old son, Pat, arrived back from work. He asked what we were watching, and after telling him, he asked that I give him the DVD when we were finished. I did just that, and the following night, after work again, he came home and talked to me for one and a half hours about the film. He said, "That was the best movie I have ever seen. It was so inspiring that I've got to show all my friends." So, what was it about this movie that inspired a twenty-two-year-old?

Finding Joe is an exploration of famed mythologist Joseph Campbell's studies and their continuing impact on our culture. Through interviews with visionaries from a variety of fields interwoven with enactments of classic tales by a sweet and motley group of kids, the film navigates the stages of what Campbell dubbed The Hero's Journey: the challenges, the fears, the dragons, the battles, and the return home as a changed person. Rooted in deeply personal accounts and timeless stories, **_Finding Joe_**, shows how Campbell's work is relevant and essential in today's world and how it provides a narrative for how to live a fully realized life or, as Campbell would simply state, how to "follow your bliss."

Pat and I talked about the "fears and dragons" we each have that get in the way of "following our bliss" and the courage it takes to do what you know is your passion. Pat is a drummer and loves music so much and yet has struggled to turn his passion into a viable career. My life has been a series of hero's journeys from building a life as a wife, mother, business owner, and teacher to ending a marriage, creating a new life, building new relationships with my adult children, and sustaining a business with Mary Anne that is an expression of my (and Mary Anne's) passion for helping businesses and individuals reach their full potential. Pat, at twenty-two, and I, at fifty-four, had something in common, and the film enabled us to connect in a way I would have never imagined.

What I know for sure is that life is a series of hero's journeys; we start off in a direction we feel compelled to follow (some of us may be thrust into the journey not always willingly or with choice). Once on the journey, we encounter difficulties that cause us to face not only our own fears and doubts but also the disapproval or discouragement from those around us, and yet, somehow, we find the courage (or determination) to keep going despite the inner and outer dragons we encounter. We return from these experiences often a little wiser, stronger, and self-confident.

Tell us about the hero's journeys you've had. Here are some questions to consider:

Where am I in my hero's journey?

What were the most powerful dragons that I've had to slay?

How was my life or I changed by this journey?

Theresa Gale

JANUARY 28, 2013

A New Twist in Decision Making

For the past many months, I've been pondering how people make decisions. For years in our sales training, I've taught, based on my belief, that coming to a decision is a very individual process. To be effective as salespeople, we need to discover how each individual, or organization makes decisions. I truly believe that it's unique to each individual and to each organization. From an Enneagram perspective, I clearly see that type certainly plays a role as well.

Decision making seems to be an area in sales that is difficult for some salespeople to master, especially now that there are so many options and price shopping is inevitable. I truly believe this new reality has impacted *how*, *when*, and *why* people make buying decisions. For sure, people are still spending money, and lots of it, but there's a new gestalt about how those decisions happen. Several weeks ago, I was having a discussion with a confidant about how I was approaching making an important personal decision. She said to me, "You've heard the saying 'decisions aren't made; they are discovered,' right?" Actually, it was a new saying to me, but, I knew in that moment that it was a spot-on statement.

This week I've been reading *The Happiness Makeover* by M. J. Ryan (a good book with a bad title). The author cites research findings on how increasing the number of options we have can actually make us feel bad about what our final decisions are in any given situation, because we have more to be regretful about because of the options we did not choose. She also goes on to say that "we are less happy with decisions because we have so many options to choose from." That too was something that I hadn't considered, yet I can see how this is an important part of the decision-making puzzle. I'm still working on what the implications of these new discoveries are in terms of sales, but I'm starting to figure it out, and those of you who I coach will be hearing more as I discover or uncover the layers of these learnings for me.

Some questions to consider this week:

- What is the cost of each choice we make?
- If we choose one thing over another, or over many others—what are we walking away from?
- How do you know which to choose?
- Does possible regret play a part in our decisions?
- What is the cost of making no decision at all?

I'd love to hear from you about this topic. In the meantime, I'm still working through my personal decision. I'll fill you in when I discover it!

Mary Anne Wampler

FEBRUARY 4, 2013

Turning a No into a Yes

I had about five things I needed to complete this week, and I found my-self diverting my attention to everything but the things I needed to get done. I noticed that, at first, my inner critic was saying, "You teach this stuff; you shouldn't have trouble getting focused?" And then, I found myself asking, "What's the next action I need to take?" and I'd do that and, again, find myself diverted onto something else. Ever have one of those days?

What I found that day, after a needed pause, was my "inner no." As I stopped what I was doing, I checked in with my head, heart, and body to see what was going on. The head was scattered, the heart was lack-ing connection to my work, and a quick scan of my body revealed that the right side of my body was clenched, tight, and almost felt like dead weight. I recognized it instantly thinking, "This is what it feels like to say no." I've been told I can be stubborn, dug into my position, and unmov-able, but this was the first time I actually felt it in me.

Coincidentally, I had listened to a talk by Tara Brach where she did a short meditation on exploring the inner experience of reactivity, finding the "inner no," and then finding the "inner yes" even if that meant saying yes to what you were resisting. So, I did just that—I said yes to my resistance to doing the things I needed to get done for a few moments, and then I felt a little release as if the unmovable was shifting, and guess what happened? I got into action and finished what I needed to do in record time.

I'm reminded of the phrase "What we resist, persists." In finding my in-ner no, I said yes to it, and by doing that, I got back on track.

This week notice when you are resisting something. Take time to pause for a bit; check in with your head, heart, and body; and if you find your inner no, say yes to it; let it be there for a few minutes, and then see what happens. Let me know if you have the same experience I did.

Theresa Gale

AUGUST 19, 2013

How Much Choice Is Too Much?

Did you know that Americans make an average of seventy choices a day?

Kent Greenfield, author of *The Myth of Choice*, and Sheena Lyenger, *The Art of Choosing*, were interviewed yesterday on Fareed Zakaria GPS, and their work reveals that when presented with too many choices, our brain becomes overwhelmed and often unable to make a choice. More importantly, when there are too many choices, we resort to tapping into our primitive brain (fight, flight, freeze) and select an option that often provides short-term relief to the discomfort we feel.

What does this mean for us? Making choices is as automatic as brushing our teeth. We are constantly presented option after option from which to choose, and our brains work overtime making decisions based on the options presented to us.

If research is correct, less is better, so it would follow that being able to limit your options will result in better decision making. Easier said than done, but give it a try; your brain will thank you!

Theresa Gale and Mary Anne Wampler

SEPTEMBER 9, 2013

Do You Have the Six Habits of Highly Empathetic People?

Years ago, Steven Covey, in his book *The Seven Habits of Highly Successful People*, got the business community thinking about the skill of empathy when he introduced the fifth habit: *Seek first to understand and then to be understood.* Then several years later, Daniel Goleman, in his work on emotional intelligence, named empathy, the ability to read the feeling of others, as one of the five components of emotional intelligence.

Well neuroscience now has something to say about the brain and empathy that we thought you'd want to know. In the article "Six Habits of Highly Empathetic People," Roman Krznaric states that neuroscientists in the last decade have identified a ten-section "empathy circuit" in our brains that, like many aspects of our brain, has the capacity to grow and change throughout our lifetime. This means that empathy is a trainable skill! All human beings are wired to be social creatures and "primed" for empathy, but not all of us have been taught to develop or cultivate this skill in our lives. Krznaric believes empathy, to become a habit, "has to be cultivated and practiced in our daily lives." In his research he finds that highly empathic people

- Have an insatiable curiosity about people.
- Challenge their own prejudices and search for what they share with people rather than what divides them.
- Expand their empathy by gaining direct experience of other people's lives, putting into practice the Native American proverb, "Walk a mile in another man's moccasins before you criticize him."
- Master the art of "radical listening," coined by Marshall Rosenberg in his work with Nonviolent Communication. Radical listening involves listening within (and being aware of our own vulnerabilities: feelings, reactions, responses) and, at the same time, being

fully present to the "unique feelings and needs a person is experiencing in that very moment."

- Create social change one interaction at a time. When one person feels heard and received, he or she, often, in turn, listens and is receptive to another, and the ripple effect of this can be transformational.
- Are non-discriminating in whom they empathize with. Everyone is worthy of empathy!

Krznaric states that he believes that "the 21st Century should become the Age of Empathy, when we discover ourselves not simply through self-reflection, but by becoming interested in the lives of others. We need empathy to create a new kind of revolution…a radical revolution in human relationships!"

Bill Drayton, the "father of social entrepreneurship," believes that in an era of rapid technological change, mastering empathy is the key to business survival skills because it underpins successful teamwork, leadership, sales, and so much more.

We encourage you to take some time to reflect on the following questions this week:

- How would you rate your ability to have empathy for others?
- How often are you able to engage in "radical listening"?
- Who in your company needs to be touched by "empathy" today? This week?
- How can you encourage the development of empathy among your employees? In yourself?

Join us in building a more empathetic workplace...we all will reap the benefits of this endeavor!

Theresa Gale

OCTOBER 21, 2013

Power and Personal Freedom

> *Between the stimulus and the response there is a space*
> *and in that space lies our power and our freedom.*
> ~Tara Brach

Are you aware of the space between? It might be the space between a colleague's comment about our work and our response to that comment, or it might be when a client calls with an issue or complaint that stems from the client's need to place blame on you or your company and our initial response to that complaint. Either way, it can feel like a full-time job to allow our attention to rest there, that is, pause, for just a few moments.

What the quote suggests is that in a moment of pause is our power and our freedom live. So often our response is automatic that we don't notice the space or give time for the pause. Sometimes the space can feel frightening: what if I don't react...what will happen then? Whatever the reason is for avoiding the pause, what is missed is the opportunity to give space to ourselves and make a conscious choice for our response. What keeps you from pausing and giving space between a stimulus and your response?

That's the question of the week. Let us know what happens when you do.

Mary Anne Wampler and Theresa Gale

DECEMBER 9, 2013

Work Directly with Your Enneagram Type to Live a More Fulfilling Life

Simply put: The Enneagram is the most effective tool we've found for catalyzing personal and professional success.

So, you know your Enneagram type. Now what? We'll help you harness this framework to create the fulfilling life you deserve.

- Start playing big. Maximize your talents so you can leverage your talents and shine brighter doing what you love.
- Navigate transitions, growing pains, and big life changes with greater ease and awareness.
- Manage your emotional reactivity, and honor yourself as you encounter sticky situations.
- Learn how to have those tough conversations with heart, savvy, and finesse.
- Drop into the deep truth of your own worth—and find big and subtle ways to express it.
- Weave it all together: zoom out to the big picture of your life, and take control of its direction. Achieve self-actualization as you create the life you want and live it with gusto.

Don't know your Enneagram type? We're also available for typing sessions to help you discover your type and get started on this life-changing path.

Theresa Gale

JANUARY 5, 2014

Practice for 2014 That Works!

Happy New Year! With only two business days under your belt, how's it going so far?

Many of you know that at the core of what motivates and drives Mary Anne and I to do what we do is the desire (passion) to increase self-awareness and self-observation in the workplace. In leadership and sales, these are vital skills that accelerate success, yet every employee, and hence the organization, benefits from learning these skills. Self-aware and self-observant individuals bring a level of intentionality to what they do and how they impact others. Workplaces change drastically when these two skills are embedded into the culture, encouraged, and rewarded by leadership.

One of the first ways to increase self-awareness and self-observation is to teach the practice of Three-Centered Awareness. Each of us has three centers of intelligence: the head, heart, and body. The head is logical; develops strategies, goals, and plans; thinks through alternatives and options; and engages in comparing, making judgments, and assumptions; obsesses over little (and sometimes, big) things; and is very active. The heart holds our emotions and feelings; it informs our thinking yet often overwhelms us or is not accessed because it is just "too much." The body is the center of instincts and sensations. The body is the vehicle through which we move and operate in the world, and it sends us information all the time, yet too often we don't listen to the body (our gut instincts); rather we let our head and/or heart rule. The goal is to access and be in alignment with all three centers.

Whether it's a daily practice of checking in with all three centers or a more intentional practice when making a decision or planning an interaction with a coworker or client, the practice is as follows:

1. Check in with your head: What are you thinking about? Where is your attention right now, and what thoughts are active in your mind? Are your thoughts about the past (what you could or should have done?) or about the future (what you need, want, have to do?)? Notice the presence of worry, judgments, assumptions, or comparisons. These can get you into trouble!
2. Check in with your heart: What's going on in your heart? What feelings or emotions are active or are you not wanting to let in? How are these feelings or emotions impacting you right now?
3. Check in with your body? What is going on in your body? Is your body tense, achy, energized, tired, and so on? See if you can scan your body and tune into what's going on. Check in with your gut. Take a few minutes to listen to what, in this moment, is going on for you.

Now let's try to practice as you consider your goals for 2014.

1. Head: What are your thoughts about 2014? What goals or plans do you have for 2014? What assumptions or judgments are you making about 2014? What thoughts will support you in 2014?
2. Heart: How do you feel about 2014? Is it going to be a good year, or are you feeling unsettled and anxious about it? What feelings or emotions will support you in 2014?
3. Body: What does your gut tell you about 2014? What specific actions will support you in 2014? How will you "know" (gut instinct) that you are on track and achieving what you want to accomplish in 2014?

We encourage you to try this practice as you kick off 2014. Don't just do it once, but incorporate it into your day, every day. A quick check in with your three centers is one way to stay healthy from the inside out!

Theresa Gale and Mary Anne Wampler

JANUARY 13, 2014

What's Going on in Your Head, Heart, and Body Right Now

In last week's Monday Morning Tip, we started off 2014 talking about the benefits of doing a Three-Centered Practice that aligns the head, heart, and body in seconds. This week we have a "real" example that highlights the value of doing this practice. Many of you shared with us your insights as you did this practice. Here's one that everyone can relate to!

As Tony sat at his desk early one morning, he began his new practice of checking in with his three centers—head, heart, and body—as he prepared for his day. As he checked in with his head, his thoughts went to an interaction that he had with his eight-year-old daughter the prior evening. He played the interaction again in his head, and as he did, he wished he had handled it differently and replayed it in his head how he would have handled it saying to himself, "The next time that happens, I'll do that." He then moved to his heart and found that he was having a reaction to the encounter with his daughter. This surprised him. He thought he had figured out what he would do the next time, so all was well, but when he moved to his heart, he felt sadness. Sadness about the way he interacted with her, about the impact he had on her, and felt that the connection with her, from his side, was "off." He then checked in with his gut and felt a sense of urgency to call her. She would be sitting at the kitchen table having breakfast, and he wanted to talk with her, so he called her and told her that he was sorry about how he had acted the night before and told her why he reacted the way he did. This resulted in him asking her to change one of her behaviors, and he promised to work on his reactions. They hung up reconnected.

Tony shared this story with me during our coaching session, and he was amazed how this small daily practice of checking in with his three centers revealed information he would have missed if he hadn't taken the time to check in. He said he would have never known or felt the sadness, and in acknowledging it and then taking action to reconnect with his daughter, he felt energized and focused for the rest of the day.

All day long we are being impacted and impacting others. With this little practice, we give ourselves permission to stop, pause, and, if necessary, declutter, unhook, and/or release unwanted or unresolved energy that gets in our way of being fully present during the day.

Tony asked me, "How frequently should I do this practice?" I suggested that doing the practice daily, even a few times a day, is important, because in doing so, you are building the muscle of self-observation, a crucial skill in leadership and personal mastery, within you. By doing so, when difficult situations arise, you'll have spent enough time in each of the three centers that when you need them most to inform your thinking, feeling, and acting, they will be ready and able to support quicker, more informed, and aligned outcomes.

So, what's going on in your head, heart, and body today?

Theresa Gale

JANUARY 20, 2014

Are You Suffering from the "I Am What I Do" Mentality?

All too often we define ourselves by what we do. In business, it's difficult not to do this, because so much is measured by the results we produce or the accomplishments we have. When we measure our success this way, we can't help but be impacted throughout the day by those individuals and situations that get in the way of success.

A recent coaching call with a business owner started with a question that resulted from an interaction with his wife. He came home one evening, and he was "down." It had been a rough day at work filled with interactions where employees didn't meet his expectations. He felt disappointed and defeated and was wondering what he was doing wrong or, more importantly, what he could do differently to get the results he wanted or needed. His wife commented how impacted he was by what goes on at work, and it made him wonder if, because he was the owner, this was just going to be the reality he would have to learn to cope with, or if maybe he was looking at it the wrong way, or if there was something he could do to shift this for himself. This is a perfect example of how the "I am what I do" mentality grabs hold of us and often gets in the way of our success.

The "I am what I do" mentality blurs the lines between the individual and the work that an individual does. If what I do is a reflection of my worth, value, or emotional well-being, then everything that happens to me in a day will impact me, and my self-confidence, emotional constancy, and energy will fluctuate based on each interaction, event, and even thought I have.

Who you are and how you manage yourself throughout the day is separate from what happens to you during the day. While situations and interactions that happen during the day are impactful, they do not need to alter your inner state; rather, if you are able to see the situation and interactions objectively (outside of yourself) and deal with them from this stance, you'll begin to make this shift. It is important to check in with yourself (use the Three-Centered Practice we've shared with you to do this) to determine what's going on for you and what specific actions you need to take. But if you find yourself, after you've dealt with the situation, thinking about it in your head, being reactive, and/or your energy or mood is altered, then the "I am what I do" mentality is running you. It's up to you to decide how long you let "it" run you!

Theresa Gale

FEBRUARY 10, 2014

Does Your Workplace Make You Feel Crazy Sometimes?

We've heard from you, and the answer is yes; sometimes your workplace makes you feel crazy.

But what is it that makes you feel crazy? Well, in our experience, it begins with "them"—they do, you know, the people who you work with. But, if truth be told, it's really about our reaction to "them" that makes us reactive and feel crazy, so we need to look at that and a few other ways the workplace makes us feel crazy at times and then learn a few strategies for how to make it a little less crazy for each of us.

Our reactivity is the cue that something has gone awry. The question is what triggers your reactivity? Here are a few cues that we've heard people tell us create reactivity in them.

The first clue that we are being reactive is when our attention goes to the "other" and gets fixated on what the "other" has done. In these situations, it is best to pause and ask yourself, "Why am I having a reaction to [fill in the blank]?" You may discover that your reaction has nothing to do with the "other" but rather is a reaction you are having that is "very familiar" and a pattern that you need to fix in yourself. Regardless, it is important to follow up the first question with this one—"Is there any action I need to take?" There are times when no action is needed, but more often than not, there can be a "next step" that moves you from reactivity back into action.

Another clue is when others communicate in nonspecific, generic language that often leaves us clueless as to what others want or need. Here is a simple question that can help you focus conversations and get the clarity you need: "How were you hoping I could assist you?" (if a manager) or "What do you need, by when and do you have any specific instructions you want me to follow?" (if an employee).

A third clue is the way someone interacts and communicates with you. There are a whole lot of "parent-child" interactions going on in the workplace. You know when someone says, "Why did you do it that way?" (critical parent) and the other responds, "You didn't tell me you wanted it that way" (blaming/defensive child). When the critical parent speaks, the defensive, blaming, or rebellious child cannot help but emerge. The goal is to have "adult-to-adult" conversations with those at work so it takes both parties to monitor what "state" (parent, child, or adult) they are coming from. The "adult" response to the critical parent sounds like "I'm not sure I understand your question. Are the results not what you had hoped?" The adult remains objective and curious in his or her response and explores solutions to create win-win outcomes. Often after exploring the specific issue at hand, it is helpful to have a conversation about how to minimize these types of situations in the future and might sound like this: "Jack I'm glad we cleared that up. Can we spend a few minutes talking about how to avoid this confusion in the future?" Sometimes it's really hard to calm the "child" who wants to react or the "critical parent" who wants to criticize and show who's in control, but at the end of the day, the workplace is less crazy when adults work with adults!

This week pay attention to what you react to. What are the things that trigger reactions in you? Where does your attention go? How do you communicate when you are triggered and reactive? Taking a pause and checking in with yourself is the first step; the second is to decide what you'll do next, and that is best determined from the "adult" state.

Happy Valentine's Day!

Theresa Gale

MARCH 10, 2014

Do You Need to Tap into Your Power This Week?

PERSONAL POWER TIPS FOR THE NINE ENNEAGRAM TYPES*

If you haven't a clue what the Enneagram is or what type you are, don't worry. Read through the nine statements, and pick the one that most fits for you this week.

Type 1: Relax today. See how many times you can accept yourself and others. When self- or other judgment arises, and it will, gently remember there is perfection in each and every moment.

Type 2: What if just for today you could give yourself what you need, you know, like you do for others? What if, just today, you ask yourself, "What do I want?"

Type 3: Spend one day without a list of "to-dos." Wander through the day noticing that there is nothing that must be done right now and that things are moving quite nicely without your effort. The sun came up, and it set, and you didn't have to do one thing.

Type 4: Take a trip on the mundane train. Do all the things that you abhor doing, those boring useless things that actually need to be completed. See how you feel at the end of the day.

Type 5: Make today National Connection Day. Reach out to someone new or to an old friend, and just talk about how life is going for them and for you.

Type 6: In *self* we trust—that's today's motto. Make a list of all the people and things you trust in, and, of course, reflect on how many, many times you've come through for yourself and for others.

Type 7: OK…time to go in slow motion for the day. Make a list, follow it to the tea, pay attention to your thoughts as they jump around, and gently bring yourself back to the task at hand.

Type 8: Ah…make today a gentle day. Be soft and squishy. Share how you feel with someone you love, and let him or her see a side of you that he or she has never seen before.

Type 9: Just for today you are focused, clear, and in sync with what you want and need to do today. Watch for the need to divert yourself from *you* and your agenda, but don't be stubborn; rather, set some boundaries so that both your agenda and others' agendas are met.

Have a great week!

Theresa Gale and Mary Anne Wampler

MAY 5, 2014

At Home or Feeling Misaligned

Recently I did a search for a list of values and found one list that had 377 values listed and another with 440.

Now you are probably wondering why that matters? I was getting ready for a training session where team members were coming together to define their purpose and mission, and often I'll do an exercise that has attendees review a list of values and identify the top ten values they live by and then the top ten values that they think the company lives by. Then they work together to define the values that they, as a team, will live by. The results of this exercise are quite revealing to attendees.

If I had to go through a list of 440 values to identify what values I lived by, I'd probably not do the exercise, or I'd skim through and pick the first ten that stood out to me. But is that really the way to define the values we live by…probably not, but it's a place to start.

Personal values are deeply held views of what we find worthwhile and what motivates us to do what we do. Our values impact our attitudes and behaviors. When working with a group of individuals, our personal values may or may not be aligned with others or the company, and this may cause tension or conflict. When we are aligned with another individual and/or the company, we feel as if we have found our "home."

A company's values are those beliefs and/or behaviors that define what is important to the company. They are the guiding principles that define the culture, serve as a bench mark for decision making, and direct the actions of all members of the organizations.

What are your values, and how do you live them out day in and day out?
Look at your calendar, and see how you are spending your time. That
will give you a clear indication of what you value.

**What's missing that is really important to you but you just aren't making
time for?**

**What are your company's values, and how aligned are you with those
values?**
If you aren't sure, look at what the company focuses on, communicates
about, and rewards. Maybe one of the reasons you don't feel "at home"
at work is a misalignment of values. Check it out!

Theresa Gale

JULY 21, 2014

Did You Know This about Listening?

SOME INTERESTING FACTS ABOUT LISTENING

The next time you get ready to have a conversation with someone, consider these facts:

- Eighty-five percent of what we have learned is through listening (not talking or reading) (Shorpe).
- Seventy-five percent of the time, we are distracted, preoccupied, or forgetful (Hunsaker).
- After listening to someone talk, we can immediately recall about 50 percent of what was said. Even less is we didn't like the subject or the person! (Robinson).
- One hour later, we remember less than 20 percent of what we heard (Shorpe).
- Less than 2 percent of the population has had formal educational on how to listen (Gregg).
- We listen at 125–250 words per minute, but think at 1,000–3,000 words per minute (HighGain, Inc.).

When listening, try to suspend your assumptions, refrain from making judgments, and silence your inner chatter long enough to listen, really listen, to what the other person is saying. As Deborah Tannen, author of many books on communication, writes, "It's a sign of respect. It makes people feel valued."

Have a great week!

Theresa Gale and Mary Anne Wampler

AUGUST 18, 2014

Conscious Choice

*We can claim the future we desire and act from it now. To
do this takes the discipline of choosing where to focus our
attention. If our brains, as neuroscience now suggests, take
whatever we focus on as an invitation to make it happen, then
the images and visions we live with matter a great deal.
So we need to actively engage our imaginations
in shaping visions of the future.
Nothing we do is insignificant. Even a very small conscious
choice of courage or of conscience can contribute to the
transformation of the whole. It might be, for instance, the decision
to put energy into that which seems most authentic to us, and
withdraw energy and involvement from that which doesn't.*
~Pat Farell

What will you do this week that is significant?

Where will you focus your attention?

Theresa Gale and Mary Anne Wampler

SEPTEMBER 22, 2014

What's the Life Lesson You Need to Learn to Live a Freer, More Fulfilling Life?

This week we'd like to share with you the life lessons for each of the nine Enneagram types to learn. Our colleagues at the Enneagram Studies in the Narrative Tradition have created a brief description of what each type needs to learn to live a more conscious and freer life.

If you know your Enneagram type, we're here to answer any questions you may have. If you don't know your type, read each one of the descriptions and select the one you think most fits for you. Then call us at 301-419-2835, or e-mail us, and we can help you further explore your type.

LIFE LESSONS FOR THE NINE ENNEAGRAM TYPES (ENNEAGRAM STUDIES IN THE NARRATIVE TRADITION)

TYPE 1
To change what can be changed, to accept what cannot be changed, and to develop the wisdom to know the difference.

TYPE 2
To develop the humility that comes from allowing yourself to be loved without being needed and to have needs of your own.

TYPE 3
To reclaim the truth that love comes to you because of who you are, not because of what you do.

TYPE 4
To reclaim wholeness in the present moment by appreciating what is here and now, feeling the experience in their bodies rather than

overindulging in the story of what's happening, and accepting yourself as you are without needing to be special or unique.

TYPE 5
To reconnect to the vitality of your life force and your heartfelt feelings, realizing that ample energy and resources are available.

TYPE 6
To reclaim trust in yourself, others, and the world, and live comfortably with uncertainty.

TYPE 7
To reclaim and accept all of life, the pleasures and the pains, in the present moment.

TYPE 8
To harness the life force in productive ways, integrating self-assertion with vulnerability.

TYPE 9
To reclaim yourself and wake up to personal priorities.

Theresa Gale and Mary Anne Wampler

OCTOBER 27, 2014

Start Your Week Off with This Practice, and Watch Your Productivity Soar!

Productivity results from focus. To be focused you need to be clear about what is important. To know what is important, you need to check in with yourself daily to ensure you are working on the things that are the highest priority and get you the greatest return on your effort, time, and resources. Try this practice at the start of each day, and watch how your productivity soars!

1. Check in with your head: What's on your mind? Where is your attention this morning? (What do I have to do? What happened yesterday that I have to fix? etc.) What are the tasks that you want or need to do today? What are your thoughts about getting these done? What are you thinking it is going to take to get these done? What thoughts are supportive? Which are not? What thoughts will support you today?

2. Check in with your heart: What's going on in your heart? What feelings or emotions are activated when you think about what you need or want to get done today? What emotions or feelings need to be expressed today? What heart-to-heart conversations do you need to have today? What connections do you want or need to make today? What relationships need attention today?

3. Check in with your body: What is going on in your body? Is your body tense, achy, energized, tired, and so on? See if you can scan your body, and tune into what's going on. Check in with your gut. Take a few minutes to listen to what, in this moment, is going on for you.

4. Now from your body center, ask the questions:
   - "For this to be a productive day, what do I need to accomplish by the end of the day?" Consider the list you generated when you tapped into your thoughts and your heart.

- "Is there anything that I need to do today but I may want to put off or avoid? What can I do to ensure that I take action on that today?"
- "If I accomplish these things today, I will _____." Fill in the blank as to what the pay-off (What's in it for you?) is to get these things done.

The first couple of times you do this, it may feel like it is taking a while to do, but as you build your internal muscle for aligning your three centers, it will get easier and faster. Remember energy follows attention, and by checking in with your head, heart, and body—your three centers of intelligence—you are building a muscle that ensures you stay aware, aligned, and awake. Simply put: be present, focused, and productive!

Theresa Gale

NOVEMBER 3, 2014

Good Decision Making Requires This Practice

"In the timeless classic, *War and Peace*, Leo Tolstoy wrote that the two strongest warriors are time and patience. The power of these warriors comes from their ability to transform situations, ease pain, and provide clarity. Sometimes situations that require our patience can feel so uncomfortable, dissatisfying, and rife with anxiety that we jump to action just to alleviate the internal turmoil. But more often than not, giving yourself that extra day, week or month to digest the situation before moving forward is all you need to stay in control. And sometimes, while you're waiting, things may surface that make your decision that much easier to make.

"Time helps you to self-manage because it brings clarity and perspective to the thousands of thoughts that go swimming through your head when something is important. Time also helps you gain control of emotions that you know would lead you in the wrong direction if you were to let them drive. It's that simple. All you need to do is force yourself to wait for the dust to settle before you make a move" (*Emotional Intelligence 2.0* by Travis Bradberry and Jean Greaves).

What decisions do you need to make this week?

The best advice I've often got is "sleep on it" and see what you want to do in the morning.

Whether you "sleep on it," "let the dust settle," or "check in with your three centers before your act," know that any level of self-awareness you bring to your decision making will make a difference!

Theresa Gale

NOVEMBER 9, 2014

Don't Miss This Key Ingredient
When Setting Your Goals for 2015

This year Mary Anne is trying something different as she works with sales professionals and business owners to set their goals for 2015. While the goals are very important, it is knowing the why behind your goals that is the real ticket to your success. By all means, do your goal-setting this year, *and* make sure your goals are compelling and inspire you to move toward that which is most important and meaningful to you. For salespeople, it rarely is making more money; it's typically what that money will do to increase their quality of life, provide for their families, or help them realize a dream or goal that has never been accomplished. For business owners, it's not always about creating more success; it's typically about increasing their freedom from the business, spending more quality time with their loved ones, or growing the business so that every employee can achieve his or her personal goals and dreams.

What is the why behind your goals for 2015? Below are some questions to guide you in discovering your why. If you need help, you know where to find us!

- What key questions do you want answered in your life?
- What, if anything, feels incomplete (or missing) from living a fulfilled life?
- What would you like to move away from or release in your life?
- What do you want to move toward?
- If you had three wishes what would they be?
- If you had three wishes for others in your life what would they be?

- Knowing this will change over time but right now "What legacy do you want to leave behind?"
- Where, and, in what ways, can you contribute the most?
- At the end of the day, what matters most to you? How will your goals for this upcoming year reflect what matters most to you?

Theresa Gale

JANUARY 19, 2015

The Value of a Pause

To stop momentarily.

To give pause.

To take a break.

To emphasize a meaning.

To hesitate.

To dwell or linger.

To rest.

There is so much value in each of these meanings. Yet, many see pausing as a sign of weakness, while we see it as a sign of wisdom, strategy, and strength.

Pausing is a skill that everyone needs to develop not just for being successful at work but for living a satisfying, fulfilling life. We've all experienced the consequences of not taking a pause—unintended impact on someone, errors, and sickness, just to name a few. Research shows that we are on autopilot much of our day, so not taking a short breath and not taking time to consider the impact of our words, or actions, and internal experience is far more impactful than most consider it to be.

As you go about your day, see where you can incorporate a pause, and you too will discover its value.

Mary Anne Wampler

FEBRUARY 2, 2015

Do You Struggle Answering These Questions?

"What's your purpose?"
"Are you happy?"
"What's most important to you?"

If you are like me, you have been asked these three questions or have asked them of yourself at some point in your life.

While these are questions that lead you to do some self-reflection, I wonder if you've ever felt it difficult to answer these questions. I had about twelve hours on airplanes last week, and I got to thinking about these questions. They seem to imply that we "should" know our purpose; we "should" be happy, and when we're not, something's wrong with us; and we "should" know what's important to us even though it changes over time. Somehow these questions make us feel "less than" or not complete or "together" enough.

Asking questions about our life is a good thing, so I'm not suggesting we stop asking questions. I am suggesting, however, that we ask better questions that help us grow, develop, and live a rich, satisfying, and meaningful life. What if you asked these questions instead?

What of your life inspires or excites you? How can you do more of those things?

What moments and situations fill you with deep satisfaction and happiness? How can you create more of them?

If there was one thing in your life that you couldn't live without, what would that be? Why? What are you willing to do to make sure that one thing stays a priority in your life?

Now those are questions I can answer. How about you?

This week be mindful of the questions you ask yourself, your prospects, clients, employees, and team members. See if you can reframe them to get at the "real" issues that matter!

Mary Anne Wampler

FEBRUARY 16, 2015

What Are the Prerequisites to Achieving Mastery

The master has failed more times than the beginner has even tried.

On Saturday, I carefully watched the weather report and planned to leave Pennsylvania, where I was visiting my parents. Snow was in the forecast, and I wanted to get home before the "big event." The weather forecasters said snow would start in Maryland around 1:00 p.m., and so I left Pennsylvania at 11:00 a.m. Well, the forecast was off. I got a call from my daughter and Mary Anne saying it was starting in Maryland just as I left my parents' at 11:00 a.m. By the time I got to the Maryland line, snow was coming down furiously, and I was now engaged in an epic battle to get home. I-95 South was treacherous the entire drive, with cars sprawled all over the road and limited visibility. I kept saying to myself, "Just keep moving," and that's what I did. My usual two-hour trip had lasted five hours!

I felt inside this unyielding determination to make it home. It was unshakable and unwavering, and nothing was going to stop me from doing just that. The quote above made me think that that's what mastery is. It is an unshakable, unwavering, unyielding determination to be the very best you can be at, not just at what you do, but, who you as a human being.

There are three skills that I consider essential when thinking about mastery—focus, persistence, and discipline. One needs to be focused on the "end result" when it comes to mastery. Questions like "what are you trying to master?" "what will it look like when you get there?" and "what's in it for me to get there?" are key questions to answer. Focus requires a clear vision to sustain its attention. One might argue that there isn't an end destination for mastery; it is a lifelong journey, and to that I would agree, yet, I believe we do have a picture of what mastery looks and feels like, and that is what we need to focus our attention on. Our destination may change along the way, but we need to have one to sustain our focus and fuel the second skill, persistence. To me persistence doesn't waver when what I am working toward is so compelling and desirable that nothing can get in the way of what I am moving toward. When you answer the question "what's in it for me to work toward mastery?" you can discover your compelling reason(s), if you can get to the very core of why you want what you want.

Lastly, without discipline, mastery is not attainable. By discipline I mean a series of practices or actions that I engage in that I am convinced will help me achieve the level of mastery I desire. Whether that is a set of goals and action steps, a mindfulness practice, or an exercise regimen, or something else, identifying what you will "do" to achieve mastery is the key. Focus and persistence are fed by discipline and vice versa. Without focus and persistence, the motivation to "do" and follow through wanes. Without discipline (knowing the "right" actions or practices to engage in), it is difficult to sustain focus and persistence.

What are you trying to master these days? Do you have clear focus of what your mastery looks like? How would you rate your level of persistence? How compelling is your desire to work toward this mastery? Do you have one or several disciplines or practices that you are engaging in to work toward mastery? Take some time to answer these questions this week. If you aren't where you want to be or you've had setbacks or failures that have caused you to lose your momentum, remember failure and setbacks aren't an option along the way to mastery; they are a prerequisite!

Theresa Gale

MARCH 16, 2015

Eliminate 44 Percent of These, and Gain More Time in Your Day

What fascinates me is that people interrupted themselves
almost as much as they were interrupted by external sources.
They interrupted themselves about 44% of the time. The
rest of the interruptions were from external sources.
~Dr. Gloria Mark

Dr. Mark, associate professor at University of California, Irvine, and a leading expert on work interruptions, has performed a host of studies on the impact that interruptions have on workplace productivity. These studies found that average knowledge workers are interrupted every three minutes—nearly twenty times per hour, and when interrupted, it takes an average of twenty-three minutes to get back to complete the original task. When you add in the finding that, on average, 44 percent of the interruptions that occur are self-induced, meaning we create them ourselves, the feelings of frustration we encounter about not being able to get our work done on a daily basis are justified, and, at least, 44 percent of the time, under our control to manage.

The best way to test these results is to track your interruptions. Frequently, I have my clients do this, and the results are always insightful. Yes, there are a host of external interruptions that occur—clients calling or e-mailing with a request, employees asking questions, or a colleague needing some information—but, knowing how you interrupt yourself is the place to start if you want to feel in greater control of your time. So how do we interrupt ourselves? With our e-mail notification turned on, we look at every e-mail when it comes in; in the midst of a task, a thought pops in our head, and we shift our attention to something else; we check our smartphones for messages every time we hear the message alert go off;

or when working on a task, we feel bored or stuck with the current task at hand and decide to do something else, just to name a few.

How can we reduce the number of self-imposed interruptions? When working on a task, commit to stay focused on a task until it is completed. This will take mental discipline, that is, not engaging other ideas or thoughts until the task at hand is completed; control of your physical environment by turning off notifications, beeps, and rings; and coordination with your coworkers and employees to hold their questions until you finish a specific task or project. So, here's what to do: Create "focus time" for yourself in one- to two-hour increments. Ask your coworkers or employees to hold their questions or needs until you complete your focus time. Turn off your e-mail and smartphone alerts (yet check them every hour on the hour for emergencies, if you need to), and let messages go into your voice mail. It may feel awkward at first, but, once you see what you can get done without external or self-imposed interruptions even for thirty minutes, you'll want more of it!

Try it this week and let us know how it works for you.

Theresa Gale

OCTOBER 5, 2015

What Fuels Increased Energy and Effortless Work?

I was recently in a sales training session with a president, who leaned over to me during a short break and said, "This is really your vocation, isn't it?" In my most "of course voice," I replied, "Why? Yes, it is. Are you just figuring that out?"

If you have been working with me lately, you know that I've been paying specific attention and giving enormous value to the development of emotional intelligence in sales and leadership. Since internal motivation is a key component of emotional intelligence, I've been asking groups of salespeople to share what they are most passionate about in their work, besides the obvious—making money. It has been somewhat surprising to me just how quickly and clearly the most successful salespeople are able to name their personal driving motivations.

Think about it: it makes total sense that we will reap greater rewards when we are guided and energized by that which we are most passionate about. When energized and focused on the pursuit of your passion, even in the most difficult, challenging times, it can feel like you aren't even really working. Remember the saying "Do what you love, and you'll never work a day in your life"? Well, there's a great deal of truth to that.

My backyard garden is a simple example. The time I spend tending it often doesn't feel like the hard physical work it can be. It can actually feel like I'm feeding my soul when I'm digging, tugging, pruning, and cultivating. This morning, before the rain set in for the day, I went out and tended the garden while pondering life and business. The gardening seemed effortless, and I was reminded just how critical it is to first know, and then remember, what motivates your work.

Sometimes my "real job" of consulting and selling can feel like a bit of a heavy grind. There are tasks I just don't like to do—for example, keeping up with what needs to be scheduled is a real pain to me. However, there's seldom a moment, even on a difficult day, when I wouldn't be energized by strategizing a deal, hearing about the wins of my clients, being there to support them, and helping them move toward their ideal vision for their company—that's what I am most passionate about!

When I work from this place of passion, I seem to say just the right thing at the right time. I see the real problems and their solutions more clearly. The results come easily, and the effort doesn't feel burdensome. Yes, it is clearly a good thing when I'm in tune with my passion. I just wish someone would schedule for me!

What about you? Do you know what, in your work, gives you energy and what doesn't? Do you know what motivates you and drives you every day? Connect to that at the start of each day, and see how your work shifts to feeling effortless and energizing.

Mary Anne Wampler

OCTOBER 19, 2015

Collaborative Intelligence Emerges as Vital in Breakthrough Thinking

Just when you think you have mastered emotional intelligence, another kind of intelligence has emerged called collaborative intelligence, or CQ. After more than fifty years of research, authors Dawna Markova and Angie McArthur, in their book *Collaborative Intelligence: Four Influential Strategies for Thinking with People Who Think Differently*, define collaborative intelligence as the measure of our ability to think, collaborate, and innovate with others.

Mastering collaborative intelligence, the authors say, requires four essential strategies. They are as follows:

Mind Patterns: Your mind pattern is the way you process and respond to information. We need to learn how to identify and maximize our own mind pattern and then be able to recognize the mind patterns of others. There's a quick little test in the book that helps you do that.

Thinking Talent: These are the specific ways of approaching challenges that energize your brain and come natural to you. The book helps you identify your talents, as well as your blind spots, and, then, once again, recognize other's talents and blind spots with the desired outcome of increasing collaboration and diverse thinking.

Inquiry: The unique way that you frame questions and consider possibilities. By identifying your own preference, as well as the others around you, you open yourself to widening your perspective and becoming a better thinking partner.

Mindshare: Mindshare encompasses the mind-set shift required to generate alignment with others. The book guides you through how to aim your individual and collective attention, intention, and imagination to create and foster mindshare.

The opening quote in the Introduction states "Great minds don't think alike...but they can learn to think together." Read more about these four strategies, as well as learn a variety of specific practices that, the authors say, are key to building individual and collective collaborative intelligence in your organization.

We'll close with a review of the book by Peter Senge, author of *The Fifth Discipline*: "Everyone talks about collaboration today, but the rhetoric typically outweighs the reality. *Collaborative Intelligence* offers tangible tools for those serious about becoming 'system leaders' who can close the gap and make collaboration real."

A great read...let us know what you learn and how you apply that learning when collaborating with others.

Mary Anne Wampler

OCTOBER 26, 2015–PART 1 OF 2

What Beliefs Support Your Productivity

Mary Anne recently passed the article "7 Popular Productivity Beliefs You Should Ignore" in Fast Company and asked me what I thought of it. Given that I have taught productivity for over twenty years and have read just about every book on productivity, my interest was piqued.

The article starts off saying that the word "productivity" "implies a one-stop solution for everyone, like we're all just churning out the same widgets." I couldn't agree more. I have worked with so many people who strive to be productive, yet, they struggle to follow through on ideas they get from books, seminars, or mass-produced calendaring systems. Trying to follow someone else's system, plan, or ideas of what productivity should be is, well, insanity. There is no one-size fits all solution; rather, in my experience, a *personalized* productivity plan is what really works. When starting from that approach, success is possible but not ensured. To be successful, you need to first identify your beliefs about productivity. The author provides a list of seven beliefs, purported by known experts on productivity, that she thinks should be ignored and substituted with a different set of beliefs. I've summarized the seven beliefs below:

- **"Search" (in your e-mail) eliminates the need for an equal filing system.** The author suggests using subject folders rather than the Search feature. Folders organize e-mails and speed up searching when done in the folder versus a generic Search.
- **Set priorities.** "You don't set priorities, you have them," says David Allen, author of *Getting Things Done: The Art of Stress-Free Productivity.* "Clear the air so you can recognize them," he says.
- **Start your day by looking at your to-do list.** The author says this is a terrible time. Do it at the end of the day for the next day. Start your day off and running, not planning.

- **Take regular breaks.** "Don't force or delay a break if it doesn't feel natural." Go with your own flow when working and manage your energy.
- **Take immediate action.** Handling everything that comes your way immediately keeps you in "reactive" mode. Use your goals and priorities to guide what and when you work on tasks.
- **Manage your time.** You don't manage time; you manage attention.
- **Touch each piece of paper only once.** Lisa Zaslow, founder of Gotham Organizers, a New York City-based professional organizing firm, says this is impossible. She says, "instead of reading, tossing, or filing mail, for example, let it stack up until you have appropriate time and energy."

I wouldn't say that I disagree with anything on this list except I am really curious as to why the author listed the first belief as #1. Of all the items on the list, that one wouldn't even make my top ten list. Regardless, this article did get me thinking about my list of beliefs that support my own productivity. If we agree that each individual needs to define what productivity is for him or her, then it would follow that each individual needs to identify his or her beliefs about productivity first and make sure that those beliefs support a personal productivity plan that is realistic and achievable.

This week look at the results you are getting. If you aren't happy with them, I encourage you to pay attention to the beliefs you hold about achieving those results and what it will take to achieve them. The beliefs we hold create the behaviors we perform, and that's where being productive or not comes in. What beliefs do you have about being productive? Where did you develop those beliefs? Which beliefs support the level of productivity you desire, and which ones don't? What beliefs do you need to change, get rid of, or reframe? Remember, beliefs create behaviors, and the right behaviors create our results!

Stay tune next week for the list of beliefs that support my personal productivity.

Theresa Gale

NOVEMBER 2, 2015, PART 2 OF 2

What Beliefs Support Theresa's Productivity

Last week we talked about the beliefs that support or get in the way of our personal productivity. The article, *7 Popular Productivity Beliefs You Should Ignore*, got me thinking about my beliefs about productivity. I shared my belief that a personalized productivity plan is what really works, and, to do that, you first have to be sure your beliefs about productivity support you in achieving the results you want to achieve. I said I'd share my beliefs with you this week so here goes.

BELIEF #1: SELF-AWARENESS OF MY STYLE AND PREFERENCES IS THE FIRST STEP TO BEING MORE PRODUCTIVE.

I tend to be more productive in the morning. I don't like to work under pressure. Creating a list of what I need to do helps me focus. I get scattered when I haven't taken the time to break down a project into smaller tasks. Knowing these things about myself and then setting up the work environment, schedule, processes, and behaviors that best facilitate "flow" for me is what supports my productivity.

BELIEF #2: I *CAN* CONTROL WHAT I FOCUS ON IN ANY GIVEN MOMENT.

Focus is a learned discipline. There are so many distractions that can grab my attention at any moment. Learning to focus and direct my attention is a must for my productivity. Having goals, setting priorities, and making task lists help me stay focused. If I don't do these things, what I know to be true is that I will lose focus. Catching myself sooner rather than later when I am unfocused, distracted, or unproductive and then knowing how to get back on track is a discipline and practice to be learned and developed.

BELIEF #3: WHEN I'M BEING UNPRODUCTIVE, I TAKE TIME TO STEP BACK, PAUSE, AND OBSERVE WHAT'S REALLY GOING ON.

This belief builds on beliefs 1 and 2. Sometimes my unproductiveness isn't about my style or preference or focus. Sometimes it's about what I'm working on and who I am doing it for. Sometimes my unproductiveness can be about the "other." That is not to say that I blame them for causing me to be unproductive, but I have learned that I can be impacted by another's lack of personal productivity.

When this happens, I need to step back and pause for a minute to see what is really going on. Am I in reactive mode and not addressing an issue that needs to be addressed? Is there something I need to say or do about the situation I am in or do I need to make a request that can set us both back on track? What I know to be true is that when I feel as if my work is being impacted by another, I lose motivation, get irritable, and I may become stubborn or passive aggressive. I can avoid this by paying attention to the signals and cues that I may be losing motivation, getting irritable, feeling stubborn, or numbing out, and I can then regroup by stepping back, pausing, and observing what is really going on for me and then get back into action.

BELIEF #4: MY INNER TASK MASTER GETS TIRED AND NEEDS A BREAK EVERY ONCE IN A WHILE.

I used to be able to do all-nighters and drive myself to plow through work even when I was exhausted. I can't do that anymore. Taking time to get away from work—resting, exercising, or doing something to clear my mind—is the best thing I can do sometimes. Relaxing the inner task-master and giving her permission to rest or take a break is not just a kind thing to do; it increases my creativity, focus, and results.

BELIEF #5: SOME DAYS JUST ARE NOT GOING TO BE PRODUCTIVE, AND THAT'S OK.

I was an all-or-nothing kind of person for a long time. What I mean by that is if I did something, I had to do it 100 percent of the time or I considered myself a failure at it. One year, I set a goal to exercise every day. Guess how long that lasted?

I've learned to let go of the expectation that every day I "should" be productive. Some days I don't feel like driving myself so hard. Some days I need to spend down time or research time so that I'm able to work on a task or project the next day. Some days are filled with unexpected issues, problems, and demands. Some days, I am my own worst enemy, allowing one distraction after another to pull my attention away from work. What is important isn't that I get my task list done every day but that I stay aware of the choices I am making in the moment and define a successful day not only by what I did but also by how in tune I am with myself and to what really matters that day. If I do this, I typically get done what is most important, not what I think "should" be done.

So, what are your beliefs about being productive? Did you discover them last week? Which ones did you change, get rid of, or reframe? Share your beliefs with our <u>Facebook</u> community so that we can learn from each other.

Have a great week!

Theresa Gale

NOVEMBER 30, 2015

A New Way to Look at Goal Setting

It's that time of year again—time to set goals for the New Year. Whether we are setting goals for an organization, a department, or an individual, neuroscience offers insights that can improve our success with this annual ritual.

Research shows that people have one of two broad motivation preferences. Either they like to *move away from* a problem, focusing their goals on avoiding what they don't want, or they like to *move toward* a vision of the future, focusing their goals on attaining or creating something new.

Knowing your motivation preference can help you when setting goals. Studies of the brain reveal that different parts of the brain are activated with each of these preferences and that our brains are hardwired to return to our habitual preference more frequently after we have set our goals. Thus, while we may include both what we want to *move away from* and what we want to *move toward* in our initial goal-setting, the reality is that once we set our goals, our attention tends to go more strongly on one motivation preference or the other, which is why we lose focus, interest, and incentive for working our goals.

What this information suggests is that if goal-setting is to succeed, we must not only include both motivational preferences in our goal-setting process but also then develop a discipline to keep activating both preferences over time in order to not lose our focus and momentum for moving toward our goals.

Try this approach when you do your goal-setting this year.

Let us know how it goes, or give us a call, and we'll walk you through the process.

Theresa Gale

DECEMBER 14, 2015

Stress and Your Enneagram Type

Transform pioneered the use of the Enneagram in the workplace, and our consultative approach makes use of this dynamic, highly accurate personality model.

The Enneagram reveals nine different "lenses," or ways of interpreting the world in which we live. We only "see" one-ninth of the truth, as there are eight other ways to view the same situation.

HOW DOES STRESS DIFFER BY ENNEAGRAM TYPE?

TYPE 1: *PERFECTIONIST*–COMPULSIVE, DEPRESSED, INDECISIVE

Becomes compulsive about work; inner critic heightens; focuses on controlling emotions; anger rises; black or white thinking intensifies/difficulty in decision making and delegating; classic Type A behavior; fear that personal flaws will be revealed, won't measure up; depression and grief come up; question the meaning of work, which can lead to growth.

TYPE 2: *GIVER*–RESENTMENT, HYSTERIA, IMPATIENT

Thoughts of resentment; attention is on other people and what they are not doing for you; heightened, visible emotions (hysterical); may punish people for ingratitude; impatient.

TYPE 3: *PERFORMER*–SPACEY, SLEEPY, INSECURE

Spaces out, sleeps a lot; throws energy at trivia; questions self-worth; blames fate "nothing I could do about it"; unable to function at usual pace. May rev up for a period of time but then collapses (usually a physical issue arises that makes you slowdown.)

TYPE 4: *ROMANTIC*—WITHDRAWN, EXTREMIST, EMOTIONAL

Moves toward others; push or pull is heightened; can become more depressed or withdrawn; stressed about what's missing; and demands attention from others usually through expression of emotions.

TYPE 5: *OBSERVER*—FRANTIC, SCATTERED, NERVOUS

Stress is internal and may not be seen yet may withdraw even more; happy-go-lucky facade hides inner tension; nervous inner buzz of ideas and information; an inability to think clearly, to relax; feel overwhelmed with too many choices; may appear scattered and in a frantic search for quick-fix solutions to buy time and save resources.

TYPE 6: *LOYAL SKEPTIC*—ANXIOUS, INQUISITIVE, UNSETTLED

Unclear rules and guidelines create stress; increase possibility of danger; fight or flight is triggered when high levels of stress are present; overactive imagination can create worst-case scenarios and lead to unnecessary stress; seeking out advice; asking a lot of questions; full-out doing to avoid thinking where fear and doubts are.

TYPE 7: *EPICURE*—JUDGMENTAL, EXACT, NARROW-MINDED

Attention turns to comparing oneself with others; judging mind; centers on limitation or inability to have or get something; having or not having versus right or wrong; pay attention to every detail; micromanages.

TYPE 8: *PROTECTOR*—INVINCIBLE, STRONG, DEPENDABLE

When stress, anger, and control issues are heightened; may withdraw as stress continues to increase; high tolerance for stress and may appear to thrive in it; feel as if they can handle anything;

denial of the stress until comes out physically and often results in "pulling away" unable to recharge. Feeling vulnerable or exposed can cause withdrawal.

TYPE 9: *MEDIATOR*–PARALYZED, NUMB, DEFEATIST

Feels a sense of paralysis—so much to do but can't do anything; deadlines create stress and so does having to oppose people openly; may look comfortable but may be numbed out; obsessive thinking and focusing on worse-case scenarios; thinking about how to get "out" of situation; often shifts blame to others; feels taken advantage of yet had difficulty taking action for self.

Theresa Gale and Mary Anne Wampler

DECEMBER 23, 2015

MARY ANNE'S BONUS REFLECTION QUESTIONS FOR 2016

A few weeks ago, Theresa penned an article called "A New Way to Look at Goal Setting," and now Mary Anne adds her list of "Bonus Questions for 2016" to the goal-setting mix.

What brings you joy on a daily basis?

What do you long to have more time for?

If you had three wishes, what would they be?

Is there something you've dreamed of doing yet feel like it might never happen?

Is there anything you need to "let go of" to be happy? (Examples—resentments, worry, expectations from someone)

What does play look like in your life?

What do you hope your kids, spouse, friends would say about you when asked the question, How did (insert your name here) live his or her life?

Where and in what ways can you contribute the most?

Mary Anne Wampler

JANUARY 4, 2016

Ninety Percent of Top Performers Have This; Do You?

WHAT IS EMOTIONAL INTELLIGENCE?

> *Emotional Intelligence is the ability to perceive emotions,*
> *to access and generate emotions so as to assist thought,*
> *to understand emotions and emotional knowledge,*
> *and to reflectively regulate emotions so as to*
> *promote emotional and intellectual growth.*
> ~Mayer and Salovey

WHY IS EMOTIONAL INTELLIGENCE IMPORTANT?

- Ninety percent of top performers have high emotional intelligence (EQ).
- EQ is responsible for 58 percent of your job performance.
- People with high EQ make $29,000 more annually than their lower-EQ counterparts.
- Executives who fail to develop self-awareness risk falling into an emotional-deadening routine that threatens their true selves. Indeed, a reluctance to explore your inner landscape not only weakens your own motivation but can also corrode your ability to inspire others.
- The development of EQ not only is necessary for solving interpersonal conflict but also serves to increase leadership credibility, generate buy-in, help to build consensus, and discover what is behind your high-performing employees.

FIVE COMPONENTS OF EMOTIONAL INTELLIGENCE

(1) **Self-Awareness:** The ability to recognize and understand personal moods and emotional drives, as well as their effect on others.

(2) **Self-Regulation:** The ability to control or redirect disruptive impulses and moods, and the propensity to suspend judgment and to think before acting.

(3) **Internal Motivation**: A passion to work for internal reasons that go beyond money and status; a propensity to pursue goals with energy and persistence.

(4) **Empathy**: The ability to understand the emotional makeup of other people. A skill in treating people according to their emotional reactions.

(5) **Social Skills**: Proficiency in managing relationships and building networks and an ability to find common ground and build rapport.

Theresa Gale

FEBRUARY 8, 2016

The Not-So-Secret Benefits of a Curious Mind State

> *I think, at a child's birth,*
> *if a mother could ask a fairy godmother*
> *to endow it with the most useful gift,*
> *that gift should be curiosity.*
> ~Eleanor Roosevelt

I think viscerally we all know that curiosity is powerful.

Do you remember Curious George, the monkey who is the main character in a series of children's books by Margret and H. A. Rey that focus on developing curiosity?

Did you know that more than seventy-five million copies of Curious George books have been sold worldwide in many languages, including Yiddish, Afrikaans, Braille, Japanese, French, Portuguese, Swedish, German, Chinese, Danish, and Norwegian?

Have you ever wondered what that level of attraction is really about? Well, a little research shows that curiosity is a key to everything from promoting happiness and protecting your brain to enhancing achievement and creating higher levels of work performance.

And did you know...

A study in cognitive neuroscience from the University of California–Davis found that curiosity helps the brain learn new material. Quoted in an article in *Psychology Today*, Dr. Matthias Gruber, the lead author of the study, says, "Curiosity may put the brain in a state that allows it to learn and retain any kind of information, like a vortex that sucks in what you are motivated to learn, and also everything around it." This was found to be true even when the surrounding material was neither interesting nor important. The study goes on to cite curiosity as a form of intrinsic motivation that increases activity in the reward center of the brain and other areas related to learning.

I think it is a powerful insight that it's not making learning material interesting but the curiosity you bring to the material that is most important. That makes total sense and reinforces what I've always known to be true for me and my clients: that curiosity makes a difference—a huge difference—in business, relationships, and certainly in my field specialty of sales.

It's simple, really.

Curiosity deepens relationships. People are more attracted to us when we have a natural curiosity about them.

Let's take, for instance, my view on the importance of coming to each sales interaction with a hunger to discover what is driving our prospects and clients to buy our services, to find out what's really going on behind the questions they are asking and what is getting in the way of them moving forward. Since all sales have an emotional component, a deep curiosity about the emotional landscape of the human beings who are sitting across the table is profoundly powerful and allows us to connect in an open and honest way, which singularly increases our likelihood of making a sale.

The other big curiosity that is perhaps most important to me is our self-curiosity. What drives us? Why do we behave, feel, and experience the world in the ways that we do? What is my reaction to a certain person or situation really about? It's never quite as it seems—at least that's the way I see it.

The most powerful tool I've ever seen for helping with this journey of self-curiosity is the Enneagram. If you're at all curious about the Enneagram and how it might support your personal and professional success, call us to schedule time for a conversation.

Curious, George?

Mary Anne Wampler

MAY 31, 2016

Transforming Fear

Our deepest fear is not that we are inadequate. Our deepest fear is that we are powerful beyond measure. It is our light, not our darkness that most frightens us. We ask ourselves, "Who am I to be brilliant, gorgeous, talented, fabulous?" Actually, who are you not to be? Your playing small does not serve the world. There is nothing enlightened about shrinking so that other people won't feel insecure around you…As we are liberated from our own fear, our presence automatically liberates others.
~Marianne Williamson

Happy Monday morning. Today's topic is fear, and I'm curious what you think of the above quote?

It especially speaks to me when I've lost sight of my talents and my power—and also when I'm feeling my superpowers, and they feel too big, too overwhelming. I can't possibly be that person with a healthy self-esteem.

There are times when it makes a lot of sense to honor fear. That feeling that makes your skin crawl, your hair stand on end, can be there for a really good reason. Other times, we believe our fears are real when they are not. Fear can be something we conjure up to keep us from truly living a full and rewarding life.

There are also those who pretend they are never afraid. Personally, I see this as a sometimes useful, sometimes weak, form of denial. Fear is a universal experience, but what makes each of us afraid is individual and personal. Our histories, our families, our life experiences, our society all impact how we experience, acknowledge, and transform our fears.

Do you know the story of my childhood? It wasn't rainbows and uni-corns. It was beautiful and bountiful at times, and it was downright scary at others. I have a close relationship with fear. Over the years, I've learned to work with it, embrace it, and learn from it, and sometimes, I get really tired of it. Yet, when I fight fear, it doesn't usually disappear. When I welcome fear, when I accept it as a natural part of life, then I can begin to understand what it is here to teach me. I can truly say that time and time again I've found freedom from my fears through chang-ing my relationship to them.

As coaches, Theresa and I listen to and witness the power of fear in many different forms. We help people overcome the hurdles fear puts squarely at their feet. We help people identify their roadblocks and help them move those out of the way so that they, too, may be liberated from the fear of fear and all its life and career-limiting impacts.

If you feel like your fears are getting in the way of your success, your happiness, reach out to us. We may be able to help you put your fears to good use.

Mary Anne Wampler

SEPTEMBER 19, 2016

Game On

Life slows a bit in summer, but now that summer is over, vacation memories are quickly fading. Kids have taken their seats at their school desks, and there's a lot on our minds as we sit at our own desks.

We know it's time to clear the clutter from our desks and our minds and focus on finishing the year in a strong position. Now—not later—is the time to fully engage ourselves in the business of achievement.

Hopefully, we are renewed, refreshed, and ready to bring our best selves to each and every day. Hopefully, we are motivated and excited about each and every task that is in front of us. Sounds like a tall order, out of reach, and not quite your reality? Well, some days it is a very tall order, and some days we achieve more than we could ever imagine.

My advice for how to bring our best selves is simple and not always easy—go with the flow. Stop beating yourself up for the days that get away from you. It's of no help whatsoever.

What is helpful is to include activities in your weekly calendar that magnify your energy levels. Perhaps for you that might be a brisk walk with your dog, working on that one project that totally jazzes you, or a good nap, if your company is progressive enough to allow that.

I always find the best step for me is to reengage my brain in something intellectually stimulating. For instance, you can always review and refocus on important year-end goals to make certain you are well on your way to success. This can also be a perfect time to bring your team(s) together to renew focus and to remember to fully engage.

Game on…let's go team!

PS: Most importantly, incorporate fun into your daily equation. Life is way too short to live without it!

Mary Anne Wampler

OCTOBER 23, 2016

Build Trust in Others by Increasing Your Conversational Intelligence

Think about the last conversation you had with a coworker. How did it go? Did you walk away feeling positive about the interaction, or did you leave feeling as if you weren't on the same page? (Last week's video on Conversational Intelligence might offer some insights into the outcome of last conversation. If you didn't watch the video at http://transforminc.com/2016/10/engaging-in-conversations-can-increase-your-intelligence/, take a few minutes to watch it.)

The author of *Conversational Intelligence*, Judith Glaser, defines conversational intelligence as "The intelligence hardwired into every human being to enable us to navigate successfully with others." She says, "Everything happens through conversations." If we want to increase our effectiveness with others, we need to understand what goes on in our brain during conversations and how these responses and reactions either support or hinder us as we interact with others.

The importance of building trust during conversations is one of the big takeaways I got from this book. The author states that within the first seven seconds of conversation, the brain registers trust or distrust, and this reaction has a significant impact on the effectiveness of the interaction. Study of the brain reveals that *if* distrust is triggered in those first seven seconds, the reptilian/old brain—and specifically the amygdala—is activated. This triggers a fear response that causes us immediately to go into fight, flee, freeze, or appease mode. When this happens, we are not able to process what is being said and are not able to be fully open and receptive to what the other person is saying. Conversely, if trust is triggered, the prefrontal cortex is activated, causing not only our brain but also our heart to be open and receptive and enabling us to engage in a collaborative and productive conversation.

So how do you activate the prefrontal cortex and not the amygdala during conversations? While our nonverbal communication has a significant role in triggering trust or distrust, our words, if chosen wisely, can contribute greatly to building trust in conversations. Here are some words and phrases that help shift distrust to trust.

Words or Phrases That Lead to Distrust	Words or Phrases That Lead to Trust
Yes, *but...*	Yes, *and* say more about that...
Why did you do it that way?	*Help me understand what* led you to do it that way?
Just *do as you're told!*	What would *you* recommend?
You don't need to know why!	*What* information do you need to help you succeed at doing your job?
You *always* mess up!	Let's talk about *what's getting in your way.*
So far, *I haven't heard anything worthwhile.*	*Help me to understand* what is important about...

This week, watch what goes on for you during interactions. When is distrust or trust activated in you? What happens to you when distrust or trust is activated? Try using some of the "trust" phrases when interacting with others and see what happens.

Remember "everything happens through conversations." What you say and how you say it really does matter!

Theresa Gale

OCTOBER 3, 2016

How Being Drafted by Major League Baseball Is Like Working with Transform

HOW BEING DRAFTED
BY MAJOR LEAGUE
BASEBALL IS LIKE
WORKING WITH
Transform

It is rewarding when you help someone go after a dream and then see it come true. I am blessed to have two different jobs that allow me to help people on their journeys to accomplishing their dreams.

As a mother (Job 1), I helped two of my sons, Kevin and Daniel, accomplish their dreams of playing baseball in college. Then this June, a few weeks after graduating from college, my son Kevin's lifelong dream came true: he was drafted by the Los Angeles Dodgers in the Tenth Round of the 2016 Major League Baseball (MLB) draft. No one in our family—or in our large circle of baseball friends—had ever been drafted. It was a wonderful moment that I will never forget!

What Kevin accomplished is very inspiring to me. What stands out most is that even when Kevin was doing really well, he continued to work hard to get better. He was focused on his goal. When challenges came up, if he struggled hitting or had a nagging injury, he did not get discouraged.

He reached out to others to get assistance, advice, and insight. This is a commonly accepted practice in the sports world—continuous improvement. Athletes consult experts to help them during the challenging times and when things are going well. They seek out coaches, trainers, doctors, and other players who have similar experiences.

As a Transform employee (Job 2), I've seen firsthand the truly amazing clients who, like Kevin, had a vision for their business or career and who have worked very hard to excel and achieve success. While seeking expert help is not as common in the business world as it is in sports, these clients have hired Transform because they want to continue to improve, and they are not afraid to reach out for help, advice, and counsel. That inspires me every day.

I've spent many years helping my sons reach their dreams. Now, I am honored to do the same working with Transform, supporting Theresa and Mary Anne in giving their best to clients who are working to be their best.

I look forward to meeting and talking with all of you, and I will keep you updated on Kevin's journey with the Dodgers.

By Christine Lachance, Marketing Specialist at Transform, Inc.

OCTOBER 31, 2016

Can You Hear Me Now? Three-Centered Listening

Listening is key to being successful in just about everything, especially relationships, and relationships are key to leadership success. One way to think about listening is through the three centers of intelligence—head, heart, and body—that are central to the teachings of the Enneagram.

Let me give you a really quick breakdown on the three centers, which each encompass three Enneagram types. Remember while we each access all three centers of intelligence, usually we lead with one.

The *heart* center (Types 2, 3, 4) is also known as the image center. These Enneagram types are concerned with image and prestige; therefore, how they are seen by others matters greatly in how they feel about themselves and how well they navigate the world.

The *body* center (Types 8, 9, 1) is also known as gut types. These Enneagram types know the joys and sorrows of physical instincts. They actively take in clues from the kinesthetic world through physical sensations and the body.

The *head* center (Types 5, 6, 7) pays great attention to thinking things through in a logical metal process and often likes planning and knowledge.

Now, let's take a look at how the three centers listen differently.

The head listens for information. Facts and logic are important parts of the puzzle. Questions these types may ask include the following: Give me the background on it. What's the strategy? Where's the problem? Where are we going? How will we get there?

The heart listens for connection. Emotional Intelligence is key. What's the emotional impact going to be? How's so and so going to feel about it? How will our image be impacted? What will people say? These are a few questions head-center types may be looking to achieve clarity on.

The body listens for concrete action and movement. No excuses here: What's the deadline? Who is doing what? How will it happen? What's everyone's gut saying about this? With these types, the body is taking in the information needed to move forward.

It's pretty clear that we are all listening for different input and that we might be missing the real message in a conversation if we don't pay attention to all three centers. So, next time you are practicing your communication skills—listen up! Remember to listen with an ear to all three centers of intelligence—you'll be smarter and a better leader for it.

Mary Anne Wampler

NOVEMBER 14, 2016

It's That Time of The Year Again...*Are You Ready?*

It's that time of the year again—time to set your 2017 goals. Why do we do this year in and year out? Neuroscience and motivation theory answer this question and offer insights into how we can improve our success with this annual ritual.

Motivation is energy that is focused toward something that we want to accomplish or attain that has a perceived benefit or outcome. Research shows that people have one of two broad motivation preferences. Either they like to move away from a problem, focusing their goals on avoiding what they don't want, or they like to move toward a vision of the future, focusing their goals on attaining or creating something new.

Knowing your motivation preference can help you when setting goals. Studies of the brain reveal that different parts of the brain are activated with each of these preferences and that our brains are hardwired to return to our habitual preference more frequently after we have set our goals. Thus, while we may include both what we want to move away from and what we want to move toward in our initial goal-setting, the reality is that once we set our goals, our attention tends to go more strongly in one motivation preference or the other, which is why we lose focus, interest, and incentive for working on our goals.

What this information suggests is that if goal-setting is to succeed, we must not only include both motivational preferences in our goal-setting process but also then develop a discipline to keep activating both preferences over time in order to not lose our focus and momentum for moving toward our goals.

Why do you do goal-setting? What do you want to move away from in 2017? What do you want to move toward?

This year we've created a reflective, thought-provoking, and action-oriented goal-setting process. If you want to get your hands on this program, reach out to us at info@transforminc.com.

Theresa Gale

NOVEMBER 21, 2016

Finding Gratitude When Times Are Tough

Brother David Stendl-Rast's book on gratefulness is a classic. In it he says, "The root of joy is gratefulness. It is not joy that makes us grateful; it is gratitude that makes us joyful."

How is it possible to be grateful or joyful during tough times in our lives? We've all had those moments where feeling grateful is the last thing on our mind when we are experiencing a loss; suffering with pain, a disease, or an illness; watching a loved one suffer; or the many other situations that arise to dampen our life spirit. In moments like these, is it really possible to be grateful, even, joyful?

I've always been a "cup half full" type of person, so I've been able to see the upside of many of my difficult moments, but that doesn't mean I don't feel the reality of my situation and the feelings that accompany it. In years past, I may have passed right by "negative" feelings to thinking of the upside of the situation I was in, but not anymore. What I've learned is that by acknowledging where I am in the present moment and letting the feelings "have a voice," I am actually shortening the window of how impacted I am by a difficult situation. Studies show that if you stay with a feeling, that is, feel it, acknowledge it, accept it, and appreciate it, for ninety seconds, the feelings will dissipate. What I've found is that if I do this, gratitude appears.

As you approach Thanksgiving Day, take a few minutes to reflect on where you are as it relates to being grateful and feeling joy in your life. If you are not quite there, take a few minutes to sit with where you are. Acknowledge where you are. Name and accept what you are feeling. Stay with the feeling for a bit, and listen to what it has to say. Remember if you stay with the feeling, it will only last about ninety seconds. As it dissipates, watch what happens; my bet is a little bit of appreciation and gratitude will arise. Maybe not joy, but definitely gratitude.

With Gratitude from all of us.

Theresa Gale

DECEMBER 12, 2016

Trust Me

This week's MMT was supposed to be about victories, but I couldn't get motivated to write specifically about that. So, I'm changing the topic to one I have a great deal of passion about, relational trust. Let's see if I can somehow tie that into victories.

Parker Palmer says, "Relational trust is built on movements of the human heart such as empathy, commitment, compassion, patience, and the capacity to forgive."

I'm not sure I have much to add to that clear, concise, and accurate statement, but I'll give it a try.

We know that trust has to be built over time and that it can be dismantled in a New York nanosecond. When we say we are going to have a heart-to-heart talk with a friend, a coworker, a client, we know we are going to speak from a place of vulnerability, and that can be downright scary.

How might our relationships both personal and professional fare if we pay close attention to each area of his quote? Let's take a look. Can we really feel what the "other" is feeling? Perhaps not always, but we can always be willing to ask—and to listen. Can we have compassion and patience with our colleagues and those close to us? Of course, we can if we show up with the intention to do so.

Do we know what it means to sincerely forgive? I'm pretty good at a few of the areas, but the vulnerable thing and the ability to fully forgive are still elusive in my desire for mastery of all things human. Oh, that's right; I'm human—no argument from anyone about that.

Parker says it's the movements of the heart that build relational trust, so I'll take that movement to mean if we come to each important relationship with a willingness to move toward each other, that will count for something. And all those small somethings may lead to one big victory for us, our colleagues, and our clients. Trust me.

Mary Anne Wampler

DECEMBER 26, 2016

Resolve

> **Resolve,** *noun*
> *1. firm determination to do something.*
> *"She received information that strengthened her resolve"*
> *synonyms: decision, resolution, commitment*

So here we are again—at the end of one year and getting ready to plan for the next.

I'm about to take my annual winter break. My birthday is on December 23, so allowing myself to take a break feels like a present I give myself. I seriously go off the grid; take time for self-reflection, dream, and play; and then set my goals and intentions for 2017 near the end of my break.

This year I am filled with gratitude for a wonderful 2016. I am full of hope for a bright future and hope you are, too. I am reminded that my vision for the future is something I help manifest through my end-of-year visioning process. (Yes, I do use the Transform Process!) I love the envisioning part of the process. It's heartfelt, creative, exciting, and inspiring.

The next part of sticking with my goals seems to be a little more difficult. Keeping up enough resolve to make things happen over time can be challenging for me, as I know it can be for many. My personal experience shows that my resolve ebbs and flows throughout the year based on both external demands and how I am feeling energetically and emotionally. This year I'm going to be keenly aware that resolve is necessary for achievement of my dreams. This year I promise myself to not have guilt about what should—or shouldn't be—on my goal list. The big change I'm committing to is that this year I will only set those goals where I believe I'll have enough resolve to sustain my focus and enthusiasm to make them happen.

I'll fill you in on how it unfolds.

Mary Anne Wampler

JANUARY 16, 2017

Cultivating Accountability

In *The Ultimate Guide to 2017: Envisioning an Awesome Year*, we guide individuals through a seven-step goal-setting process. Each step builds on the previous one, and the process culminates with creating and then implementing an accountability plan. Putting your goals in writing is one step toward accountability, but what really seals the deal is a clearly defined plan that you design to hold yourself accountable throughout the year.

Most people set goals and even write them down but often resist holding themselves accountable. From years of working with individuals, I think everyone struggles with accountability to some extent. It all comes down to what is driving our resistance to being accountable and if the pay-off for being accountable is compelling enough for us to overcome that resistance. For me, in the past I've rationalized that it's so much easier to not commit to something (a goal) or not tell others my goals. That way, if I don't achieve them, I won't be embarrassed or I won't disappoint others if they were counting on me to achieve those goals. That rationalization comes down to avoiding conflict, which has been my lifelong strategy to stay safe and keep the world harmonious around me. But what I have learned, often the hard way, is that when I don't hold myself accountable and achieve my goals, the only person who really is impacted, disappointed, and left living a more reactive rather than a more intentional and fulfilling life is me.

Years ago, I worked with a coach who helped me realize that I could change this behavior for myself by first identifying what I really wanted for my life. Some of Mary Anne's questions in our goal-setting guide are great ones to ask to discover what you really want. For example: What brings you joy? What have you always dreamed you wanted to do but never make time for? What do you want your legacy to be? What, if anything, feels missing (or incomplete) from living a fulfilled life?

Once I know what I want, I can then zero in on setting some goals to achieve it. As the steps indicate, identifying significant achievements (milestones) along the way gives me bench marks to know if I am making progress toward my goals throughout the year. But unless I develop an accountability plan, that is, that I've looked at what specific actions I will take; how I want to allocate my time, resources, and energy in the new year; how I will handle resistance if it arises; and how I will keep myself motivated throughout the year, the likelihood that I will achieve my goals becomes significantly less.

Don't leave 2017 to chance; take the extra step to secure your success by developing your 2017 accountability plan. I'm building mine. How about you?

Theresa Gale

MARCH 20, 2017

Set Your Internal Navigation for Success in 2017

The first quarter is done. The results are in, and we're looking to the second quarter. In three short months, we will be halfway through the year. Time is truly flying by, and we don't want reaching our personal and professional goals to fly by, too.

Kicking off goal-setting for 2017 was a little delayed this year for many of my clients, while everyone made a year-end push to bring 2016 results in. Then, there was a collective sigh and a needed break before getting to the business of imagining 2017. But now that our 2017 goals are set, we need to stay focused and inspired to reach them.

So, here are a few helpful tips if you happen to find yourself and your goals in the second-quarter doldrums:

1. Take a day or even a half-day self-retreat. Gather your goals in hand, go someplace you find inspiring and affirming, and review them. Reflect honestly on your progress. Are you on track? Do your goals still make sense? I believe goals are not actually set in stone. You are in charge of your life—and sometimes work—so make adjustments as it makes sense.
2. Reflect on how you are celebrating your own accomplishments. This often-overlooked aspect of goal-setting is vital to keeping your motivation and energy moving forward. What can you do to reward yourself for what you accomplish?
3. Make sure you have fun plans in your future. Take out your calendar and schedule personal time—vacations, family time, massages, acupuncture, that sort of thing.
4. Set up a peer coaching arrangement with a teammate to review milestones and provide emotional support and cheerleading.

5. Have a plan for getting back on track when you wake up to find yourself off track. For instance, if you know that having your day planned in advance helps you—plan your next day. Don't make this complicated.
6. Give yourself a break when you need it. Go for a walk. Go to the beach. Go have lunch with that friend who always makes you cheerful.
7. Remember, goals aren't achieved in a straight line. There will be ups and downs. The trick is to redirect yourself back to the course when needed.

As I close I realize that I'm writing this for me too. Let's stay the course together and make 2017 a fulfilling journey.

Mary Anne Wampler

APRIL 10, 2017

Got Relevance??

If you want to be interesting, be interested.
~David Ogilvy, *An Original Advertising Guru*

At the rate the world is changing, it's easy for a business to get lost in a crowded and ever-evolving market. The speed of change and increased complexities for a growing business create new demands everywhere. To grow a business takes vigilant attention to staying relevant to clients, prospective clients, and shareholders. I've heard it said that a business is either growing or dying but that there's actually no resting in place.

It never turns out well when a business loses its importance, loses its edge, or loses its relevance within the marketplace, and over the past year or so, I've been encouraging clients to embrace the notion that it's worth paying special attention to where they stand in terms of relevance. These conversations are always robust and fascinating.

Relevance may be especially on my mind because soon Transform, Inc., will celebrate our twenty-first birthday. I am pleased to say that we have successfully traversed and continue to navigate the winds of change. Twenty-one years after we began, staying innovative, renewed, energized, and engaged remains as important—if not more even more so—than it was the day we passionately kicked off Transform.

There's always a new frontier of challenges and opportunities for us and our clients. Remaining relevant takes a commitment from us and from our clients to serious growth, which is sometimes gut-wrenching and sometimes wholly delightful. Staying interested and passionate about business in general and your business in particular is paramount to staying relevant.

As you ponder relevance, here are some questions for your consideration. Does your company have the self-objectivity and the courage to acclimate quickly when needed? Are you nimble or set in your ways? Does the organizational ego feed itself on its own PR, or are you humble enough to keep reinventing yourselves?

Let us never forget, as Ogilvy so aptly reminds us, that it is being interested that has helped and will help to keep us interesting.

Cheers to our next twenty-one—and to yours!

Mary Anne Wampler

MAY 8, 2017

The Power of Moms

Mother's Day is upon us, and I'm thinking about the many moms I've worked with over the years. I've seen their struggles and triumphs, both in the workplace and with their kids. Quite frankly, they inspire me with their ability to get business done while wondering what's for dinner tonight and what about day care for tomorrow.

In my view, motherhood has made these women stronger employees and leaders. I've seen their decision-making abilities sharpen as they help their children with theirs. I've seen their compassion, teamwork, and self-awareness increase tenfold as they navigate motherhood. Seriously, who can sort out multiple priorities better than a mother?

These women also make the work world a better place with their "Mom" perspective. They can be tough as nails while at the same time considering the whole person, not just their value to the bottom line. Evidently, seeing yourself through your child's eyes makes you want to be a better person, and we can all learn from that.

I've also been lucky enough to watch these moms' children grow into amazing adults. I know these millennials are going to change the world, in part, because of the unconditional love from their moms and the examples their moms have embodied for them. Yes, it's good for the soul to work, it's exciting to be passionate about success, and yes, it's good to be driven to achievement.

The balancing act required of working moms is daunting, but their ability to combine work and motherhood benefits everyone. Despite the sometimes-hard days, studies show that overall the moms themselves are generally happier and more self-confident than those who don't work. The kids I know who have working moms are rewarded with life and business skills and perspective that will serve them oh so well, and the companies these moms work for profit from their hard-earned skills.

This week make sure to take a moment to notice and celebrate the gifts moms bring to your workplace.

Mary Anne Wampler

JULY 10, 2017

Still Charting Your Course in 2017?

I last checked in with you about your 2017 goals in March. Well, today is July 10, which means—gasp—the year is over 50 percent finished! Summer, sweet summer, already seems to be sliding fast into the past while vacations, concerts, family time, beaches, books, and cookouts are still on our minds, or at least on mine.

If you completed your *Ultimate Guide to 2017* goal-setting book, now is the perfect time to dust it off and evaluate if you are on target—whether you are truly charting your own course or following someone else's path, or perhaps a little bit of both. I recall, not so fondly, someone saying to me years ago, "You are either working your plan or someone else's." Oftentimes, I lose track of what's important to me because I'm giving all my attention to helping everyone else's visions come true. Because I so love doing that, I can fade into the background in my own life and forget to focus on my own goals and intentions.

I encourage you to embrace the slower-paced energy of summer: pause to revisit your dreams, reevaluate your progress, and make desired revisions needed to script the next chapter of your life!

It is said that sharing your vision is an important step in realizing it, so, here's my   2017 vision board. It reminds me of what I'm passionate about, at least for now. I hope when looking at your vision board, it will help remind you of what you're passionate about, too!

Mary Anne Wampler

AUGUST 28, 2017

What Does Human to Human, #H2H, Mean?

Social business strategist Bryan Kramer comments, "Communication shouldn't be complicated. It should just be genuine and simple, with the humility and understanding that we're all multidimensional humans, every one of which has spent time in both the dark and delightful parts of life. *That's human to human.*"

The heart of #H2H is so simple that you could miss its wisdom. It is a mind-set. It is the intentional decision to break down barriers and communicate authentically to everyone—your team members, prospects, customers, the board, and all the various people you engage and connect with—during the course of "doing" business. How? As an active listener. Why? Because humans just want to be heard. So simple.

Commit to practicing authentic listening with the people you encounter this week. Make them feel like they matter. Then, as Bryan Kramer suggests, "Invite your people to the party." Ask your team members to make a small shift in their interactions—to simply talk less and listen more. Ask them to take notes. Be sure to lead a team follow-up conversation to find out what resulted.

Be sure to explore Bryan's ideas on how to speak human via his e-book, and take a deeper dive into his book *There Is No B2B or B2C: It Is Human to Human.* The promise to break down the communication barriers and be authentic is the simplest and the most important step. Embrace the simplicity shift—to "speak human"—and you may find solutions to challenges that have seemed more complex. Remember, it is possible to move forward without having it all figured out. That's the beauty, and the brilliance, of being human.

By Elizabeth Thomas, Communications Consultant, Elizabeth Thomas Communications

Index